Here's to You, Jackie Robinson:

The Legend of the Prichard Mohawks

by Joe Formichella

with an introduction by Ron Fimrite

Here's to You, Jackie Robinson:

The Legend of the Prichard Mohawks

by Joe Formichella

with an introduction by Ron Fimrite

MacAdam/Cage

MacAdam/Cage
155 Sansome Street, Suite 550
San Francisco, CA 94104
www.macadamcage.com

Library of Congress Cataloging-in-Publication Data

Formichella, Joe, 1955—
  Here's to you, Jackie Robinson : the legend of the Prichard Mohawks /
by Joe Formichella.
      p. cm.
  ISBN 1-59692-127-7 (hardcover : alk. paper)
  1. Prichard Mohawks (Baseball team)—History.
  2. Baseball—Alabama--History. I. Title.
  GV875.P75F67 2005
  796.357'63'0976122—dc22
                                                    2005003065

Manufactured in the United States of America.

10 9 8 7 6 5 4 3 2 1

Book design by Dorothy Carico Smith

Dedicated to my father,
James Anthony Formichella,
who first put a baseball into my hands,
and into my life.
Thanks, Dad.

Introduction
by Ron Fimrite

*W*e tend now, so many years later, to take for granted Jackie Robinson's enormous contributions not only to our national pastime but also to our national conscience. Jackie is now…well…just history. There are even some exorbitantly rewarded African-American ballplayers today who are only vaguely (if that) familiar with Robinson's heroic strivings on their behalf.

The same certainly cannot be said of the Prichard Mohawks of Mobile County, Alabama. Back in the 1950s, these "itty-bitty" black ballplayers took their inspiration from Robinson's pioneering ordeal and, on their own level, mirrored his courage and fortitude. Under the extraordinary tutelage of Jesse Norwood, their team's founder and manager, they became a unifying force in a racially divided community.

The Mohawks were hardly the best ballplayers around Mobile, a city that spawned Hall of Famers Henry Aaron, Billy Williams and Willie McCovey, but they were legends in their own right. They played the game with an attention to detail and a creative energy rarely seen even at the major league level. Faithfully, they observed Norwood's sage counsel that since in baseball and life the door of opportunity stays open only so long, you'd better stick your foot in it fast.

Many of those early Mohawks are still significantly a part of life in their home city, and their touching and often-hilarious recollections of the good and even sad old times give Joe Formichella's book a singular vitality. And yet, the Mohawks and their inspirational leader are not the whole story here, because Formichella artfully weaves into his narrative the circumstances leading up to Robinson's breaking of baseball's racial blockade. Along the way, he also traces the history of the civil rights movement and the rise and fall of Negro League baseball.

For good measure, he makes a persuasive argument in support of Mobile's claim to be the nation's leading breeder of baseball talent. This is in every sense a book both rich in history and full of life. It's also one helluva read.

—*Ron Fimrite*

Here's to You, Jackie Robinson:

The Legend of the Prichard Mohawks

Baseball is the generations,
looping backward forever
with a million apparitions
of sticks and balls,
cricket and rounders,
and the games the Iroquois played
before the British came.
Baseball is fathers and sons playing catch,
the profound archaic song of birth,
growth, age and death.

— *Donald Hall*

It ain't like football.
You can't make up no trick plays.

— *Yogi Berra*

Prologue

*I*n the spring of 1948, in Mobile, Alabama, Jackie Robinson played in a preseason exhibition game against the Mobile Bears, Brooklyn's AA farm club. Robinson's Dodgers, defending National League pennant winners, were barnstorming their way north, traveling by train, readying to start the new season. The Bears had won the 1947 Southern Association crown and had some marquee players of their own in George "Shotgun" Shuba, who'd been with Robinson for his debut with the organization in Montreal in 1946 and holds a spot in the record books for hitting a World Series home run in his first major league at bat; Stan Wasiak, who would become the winningest minor league manager in history; and Chuck Connors, future television star. Fans filled the wooden grandstands and bleachers at Hartwell Field on South Ann Street. The colored bleacher section tucked out by the right field foul pole was packed. Mobile has a baseball history that goes as far back as that of any other city, and Mobilians eagerly gave up the seventy-five cents admission charge to see their Bears go up against the likes of Pee Wee Reese, Duke Snider, Ralph Branca, and Al Gionfriddo and their infamous manager, Leo "the Lip" Durocher. But the biggest draw of the day had to be Jackie Robinson, the first black professional major league player of the century and the 1947 National League rookie of the year.

The fans down along the right field line, for whom seventy-five cents was a little harder to come by, maybe, a little tougher to justify, couldn't have been kept away at double or even triple the admission price. Hometown baseball player and big league prospect Aaron Watson says he saved pennies throughout the weeks leading up to the game in order to attend. It meant that much to see Jackie Robinson. That one game, and Robinson's subsequent appearance down on Davis Avenue, electrified Mobile's black community. The flesh-and-blood Jackie Robinson, the man who changed forever how black people thought of themselves, embodied opportunity and possibility, something unknown, unthinkable in that community as little as twelve months prior to that day. For so many young boys and men in the area, that one game proved that opportunity existed. For someone like the teenaged Henry Aaron, it meant everything. It changed his life.

Jesse Norwood was not in attendance at Hartwell Field that afternoon. A married man, father of a baby boy, and not too long out of the Merchant Marine, Jesse would have been at work, though he probably listened in on the radio broadcast. He was a laborer, and his concerns were more immediate, as they had been for much of his life already—a decent day's pay, food on the table, for his wife, his first-born son, himself. But, Norwood, like Robinson, would change the lives of a generation of men, change the way a whole community thought about itself, through the game of baseball.

The correspondence of these two lives, men born less than a year apart in the Velvet Corridor of south Georgia, separated by fifty miles of dirt road whose trajectories would take them on significantly different though curiously parallel paths, is the story of *Here's to You, Jackie Robinson: The Legend of the Prichard Mohawks*. Two lives, fifty miles of highway, one game.

Baseball, they say, at the heart of it all, is a game of statistics, to the delight of some and consternation of others. Pulitzer Prize winner Bruce Catton, founding editor of *American Heritage*, wrote in those pages forty-five years ago that "[baseball] is the only pastime on earth that leans heavily on the accumulation of page upon page of inherently dry statistics."[1] But those dry statistics, laws of opposing averages, probabilities, vectors of speed, acceleration, the wind, recurring and shifting counts, lend the game a concurrence that is accomplished in other sports only with a clock. Statistics locate the game of baseball, it's true, though they never tell the whole story, and some of the game's best and most revered writers caution against an unguarded reliance on them. In his foreword to the latest, posthumous edition of Leonard Koppett's *The Thinking Fan's Guide to Baseball*, Pat Gillick tells us, "Statistics have become very important in the modern era, but the industry remains a people business. No one understood that better than Leonard. He was a pioneer in employing statistical analysis as a tool. However, as he said, if not used sparingly and correctly, the tool can do more harm than good."[2]

Later, in that same book, Koppett wrote, "Pitching is 75 percent of baseball—or 70 percent, or 90, or any other high number that pops into the mind of the speaker. The more popular current phrase, 'pitching is the name of the game,' reflects the fact that it is again more fashionable to speak in metaphors since high-powered computers have usurped the illusion of accuracy baseball statistics used to supply."[3] He has provided a necessary distinction between utility and comprehension, points on a scale and depth of measurement, between raw data and baseball statistics. What Koppett seems to have been urging, through that distinction, is a constant wariness against imparting too much importance to mere numbers, when it comes to baseball, particularly. But that caution is just as warranted in the consideration of other aspects that swirl about this story, aspects like race relations and equality, and in any "business" of "people," really, where human endeavor and human nature are folded into the mix. Equality, for one, is meaningless, statistically, in any application other than mathematics, because it is, despite being such a lofty and worthy ideal, unquantifiable. As an ideal, it can never be about balancing one tally of numbers or another. Baseball, too, suffers from any similar impulse toward purely objective comparison. There are too many undocumented statistics to factor in, for starters. As an example, there's that *other* sacrifice, which doesn't show up on any player's stat sheet: With a runner on second base and nobody out, a prime objective of the batter is to hit the ball to the right side of the field, even if that means forgoing that batter's principal strengths, even if it means grounding out, something that does a batter's personal stats no good at all, though it does provide the *team*—by moving the runner to third with less than two outs—a higher-percentage opportunity to score. It's an "uncredited sacrifice," Koppett wrote, one that "doesn't show in the statistics," but one that "managers remember and appreciate," as should fans.[4]

All of which is to say that beyond the numbers there is an interminable amount of interdependent statistics (documented or not) and hunches and patterns and mystery that course through the beating heart of baseball. And it's the same as any other beating heart. If one absolutely must, the story can be reduced to numbers, of beats per second, diastolic and systolic pressures, and ejection fractions, but that can't speak at all to what it feels like to be alive, alive and breathing. A Nolan Ryan no-hitter pitching line, which includes six walks along with the eleven strike-outs, doesn't speak at all to the defensive drama that must have occurred. In game four of the 1947 World Series, Bill Bevens pitched "the most strangely beautiful game ever seen in a World Series,"[5] but lost. Of the game, Roger Kahn says, "Nobody who saw that game or played in that game can forget it." Bevens's pitching line of eight and two-thirds innings, one hit and ten walks—two of the three Series records he set that day—is certainly curious. What's unforgettable about it is the story behind the numbers, dubbed "Cookie Lavagetto's triumph." For eight and two-thirds innings, the game—*almost* the first modern World Series no-hitter—belonged to Bevens. Then Lavagetto took it away with one swing of the bat. That's the front story. Behind that story there's a web of debate and disagreement and opinion about Al Gionfriddo's stolen base, Bucky Harris's defiance of "conventional" wisdom, Yogi Berra's pitch selection— the backstory, the folklore.

It is the folklore of baseball—the legends and stories spun from a single statistical locus at times—that illuminates the game across eras in its otherwise timelessness. Statistics and stories: When there isn't a particular number, of home runs or games played or innings pitched, at the core of any given legendary

Aaron, Ripkin, or Ryan, there is an annotative tale explicating the number, sometimes referenced only by an asterisk in the record books, but there is almost always a story.

An undocumented but acknowledged statistic holds that during the middle of the last century, across a generation from the mid-1940s to the mid-1960s—which wouldn't include the granddaddy of Mobile baseball, Satchel Paige, or the great "Double Duty" Radcliffe, who's still telling stories at 103 years old—more and better major league baseball talent came out of Mobile, Alabama, than has ever come out of any other area before or since. It is debatable, of course—and it has been debated, another of those baseball underpinnings, debating relative statistical merit: just last year Mobile's *Press Register* published comparative lists of players from the country's most prolific base-ball towns, Chicago, L.A., New York, and of course Mobile's came out on top; it may have taken a little gerrymandering, though, this is baseball, after all, and not politics—but the list of luminaries from that time is replete with Hall of Famers, all-stars, and cham-pions. Hank Aaron leads the parade, followed by Willie McCovey, Billy Williams, Frank and Milt Bolling, Cleon Jones, Tommie Agee, Tommie Aaron, Amos Otis, and others. For part of the season, at least, the entire starting outfield of the 1969 Miracle Mets were native Mobilians. Starting National League all-star teams of the era fielded more than half their players from Mobile. Years later, as a commentator, Frank Bolling would broadcast a challenge to anyone willing, that he could put together a team of only Mobile players and beat any team from anywhere else. At last check, no one has ever taken him up on that. Dizzy Dean, on his radio show, once asked Aaron, "What y'all got going in Mobile [to account for all that talent]?" Hank's famous answer, "Guess it's in the water," might be more intuitive, legendary, than dismissive. Hemmed in by water to the east and south, Mobile is wedged against a permanent backstop. The population distribution and growth pattern, from the waterfront downtown toward the west and north, looks a lot like a baseball diamond, in fact. There is the tropical climate—not unlike Cuba or the Dominican Republic, baseball breeding grounds that could rival Mobile[6]—where water hangs in the air, heavy and moist, year round, so there's never really any off-season. If you consider another Hall of Fame inductee, Ozzie Smith, who was born in Mobile and spent his first five years exposed to or ingesting the local waters, that puts Mobile at the top of that particular statistical list, raising the possibility that there must have been something magical going on. Aaron's answer is as good as any other, at the very least.

There is more to the story behind that statistic, though, more impulse to Dean's question. Any discussion with any of those baseball notables, or with the men who managed or coached them or played along-side them, doesn't proceed too far before an insistence that for every Aaron or McCovey or Williams who went from the sandlots of Mobile to Cooperstown, there were at least three or four other players with just as much talent and ability who never made it out for one reason or another. Aaron says so in his book. James Harris, godfather of Mobile baseball, who man-aged all three of those inductees at some point in their ascension, swears it's true, swears Billy Williams had brothers better than he was, swears that Moose Andrews was the best player he *ever* saw, period. Sta-tistic? Or the inflated tale from an old man, a story that's gotten oversized from half a century of telling and retelling?

There are plenty of others who will nod in tacit agreement with Aaron and Harris, and then hint that it was the whole baseball scene that was so nurturing, rather than an explosion of isolated individual talent. Baseball, they will simply say, was the thing to do, was being played everywhere there was flat ground or a cleared street.

While the baseball frenzy may have been all-per-vading, it was also often transient and without much structure. Teams formed, men allying themselves sometimes for just a weekend's worth of games, and then dissolved. Different semiprofessional leagues composed of teams spread all along the Gulf coast came together, fell apart. That satisfied the immediate desire to play but left the long-term development of some of those players unattended. Someone like Moose Andrews, who could always find a game around Mobile, suffered, ultimately, from that nomadic, hired-gun approach. At one time he was said to have been as good as or better than the legendary Josh Gibson and was signed to a professional contract, but he couldn't function within the rigors of a major league organization and quit.

And that is the point in the story where the most knowledgeable baseball people of the time will say that though there was an abundance of raw baseball talent in the area, especially in the black neighborhoods, there was also a dearth of structured support, in those same communities in particular. And then they'll go on to mention the exceptions to that rule, exceptional baseball men like Jesse Thomas, who single-handedly held together the Gulf Coast League, and James Richardson; exceptional teams like the Prichard Athletics and, especially, the Prichard Mohawks. Founded in the mid-1950s of neighborhood kids more than baseball men, lasting throughout the baseball heyday, the Mohawks would become the organizational model as well as the competitive measuring stick for other teams playing throughout the region. The man responsible for the organization, Jesse Norwood, formed the team without any known baseball experience or knowledge. He was simply looking for some way to help the kids who would congregate beyond his stoop. He managed the team until the day he died, too early, of heart complications, not too long before Jackie did. This is a story of their parallel lives, some of their statistics, but mostly the measure of the men, which can only really be gleaned from the legacy they left behind.

Unlike Jackie Robinson, the story of Jesse Norwood exists mostly in the minds of the men whose lives he changed: his son, Jesse Norwood Jr., the thirty-five or forty former Mohawks, and a host of other baseball men who credit Jesse for forcing them to elevate their game or their organization if they were going to play his. The team, like most black teams of the era, did not receive a lot of press in its time, and the records of their games, scrupulously annotated in score books, have long since fallen into ruin and been discarded. The pictures, informal snapshots taken by family and friends—because none of the national sports publications, the *Sporting News* or the brand-new *Sports Illustrated*, thought to document the team's exploits—are fuzzy, unprofessional, and have mostly slipped through the gaps of hard lives lived, family, and responsibility. But the memory of Mr. Norwood, coursing strong and true and vital in the lifeblood of these men, is very much alive, even if it has to be supplemented by unverifiable data, even if it is at times, clearly, the ethereal *stuff* of legend. The salient fact of the matter is that the otherwise unavailable influence Norwood wielded over these men changed their lives, and in some instances, saved their lives, which could just as easily have fallen through the cracks of a divided and divisive society and disappeared. And they now want to tell their story; they want to tell it, embellish it, exaggerate, probably, because they believe that even if baseball is not the preeminent pastime that it once was in Mobile, the story itself has value, redeeming value, for a new generation of black youths falling through those same cracks.

Their story, then, has certain, undeniable mythological proportions, for which I will not apologize. To me, the game of baseball itself has those same mythical qualities. It is a game of shifting and variable borders that exists out of time, in the best oral traditions of antiquity, where the historical data provide merely a framework. It is the story that matters. Here is the story, then, of two men, separated at birth by fifty miles of South Georgia plantation road, about one game. *Here's to You, Jackie Robinson: The Legend of the Prichard Mohawks.*

One

Mobile city councilman Fred Richardson, in a dark suit, over a maroon dress shirt open at the collar, stands before a crowd gathered inside the brand-new Trinity Gardens Recreation Center. The complex, with its green, expansive grounds and activity center, is still under construction, with ball fields and a swimming pool and even a gymnasium, still only sketches in the ultimate plan. It has taken the councilman some years to convince the city of Mobile to commit to the idea. The three acres of property occupy land straddling the limit between Prichard and Mobile, Alabama. It is in the heart of the Trinity Gardens community, an area of Mobile County that has seen its share of hard times. On a hill rising above all that stands a mortared brick and glass building, its tubular façade yawning over the high entry doors, fronted by a concrete basin in which one day a water fountain will gurgle in perpetuity. This is the recreation center, a testament to perseverance and persistence. The complex, not far from the intersection of First Avenue and Ruth Street, borders the remnants of the baseball field that was the home of the Prichard Mohawks.

Mr. Richardson, in his opening remarks to the gathering, speaks to that perseverance, addressing former Mohawks brought together as a unit again fifty years after the beginning of their story, some reunited for the first time in many years. "*Too* many years," they murmur to one another, exchanging affectionate embraces as they file into the assembly room. "Too many years."

"You men," Mr. Richardson says, "represent the legend that was the Mohawks. We're here in this beautiful facility, a facility that *would not have been possible* without Jesse Norwood and you Mohawks, to talk about how we can all carry on the legacy of Mr. Norwood and your baseball organization."

Those men, former Mohawks, some of them showing the effects of aging, of a harsher passage of time, more than others, nod their assurance as if they were still playing ball, imbued with the memories they planted in that ground so many years ago: standing in the batter's box, acknowledging the strategic sign delivered by hand signals from their third base coach or their manager, Jesse Norwood. They are forever baseball men, scattered about the room, covering the alleys, guarding the lines, according to their positions on the team or their responsibility within the organization.

Off the left end of the long front table Lyonel
Pugh sits slouched in a metal folding chair. His legs,
too long and lanky to fit comfortably underneath the
table, sprawl out into the aisle. Arms hanging loose at
his sides, hands open and relaxed, resting on his
thighs, he is ready, nonetheless, to react with the
reflex of muscle memory, the way a third baseman has
to if he is to avoid being knocked unconscious by a
screaming line drive or eaten up by a sizzling ground
ball defending the hot corner. At the opposite end of
the table Bennie Harris appears cautious, maybe even
a little subdued. It's hard to tell if that's the result of
the regimented lifestyle he's been forced to adopt in
the five years since his multiple bypass surgery, or if
the second baseman is just missing his double-play
partner, John Lee Cowan, who could not make the
trip from South Carolina.

Sitting left of center at the next table, the Reverend Robert Emanuel Jr., secretary, center fielder, and
field captain, has his elbows vigilantly braced on the
tabletop. Four seats to his left, dapper Sam Madison,
sporting a black leather fedora and a neat mustache,
leans back in his chair, with his legs crossed, smiling.
Another outfielder, he was known for his batting
skills and his ability to clout tape-measure home runs
on demand. Bill Dillard, a journeyman infielder, sits
by himself in the back. Standing in the rear right
corner of the room, James "Popcorn" Campbell, "the
man with the golden arm," waits. Trim, still muscular

under his business suit, nearly sixty, he'll say he's ready to pitch again, just get up the game. The team's star left-handed pitcher, Willie "Shoe" Lomax, stands at the front of the room along with Jesse Norwood Jr., the man responsible for this gathering, who had conceived the plan they were there to hear about, as well as other dignitaries, such as county commissioner Sam Jones, Jesse's cousin. Modest and quiet, the Reverend Lomax was up front to deliver the invocation.

There are even opposing teams represented in the crowd. Dr. Jimmy Knight, a Mobile County school board member, is ready to testify that the Mohawks forced everyone else to elevate their game. Jimmy played on the Hillsdale Heights team but tells of travels within the Kansas City and San Francisco organizations where he would run into players or teams who wanted to join the Mohawks or wanted Jimmy to arrange a game against them. And rival manager Earnest Hines, of the old Trinity Garden Blue Devils, sits smiling, cane on one side, great-grandson on the other, smiling back on those days of baseball with a pure love of the game.

Presiding over all this, at the center of the front table, sits Ellis May who was there from the beginning—"the foundation," as he says. He wears a navy blue Mobile City Maintenance uniform, having just come from work. "Ellis" is stenciled onto the oval, white name patch over the left breast pocket of his shirt, but everyone in the room, the other Mohawks, their families and friends, the assembled dignitaries, know him as "Candyman."

"'Cause I had them sweet, skinny legs," he explains, "that the ladies loved."

Candyman lays his hands flat against the tabletop. The ring finger of his left hand, his glove hand, crooks at an angle, and the basal thumb joint of his right hand is permanently swollen after so many dislocations. Whatever the ladies might have thought of his legs, Ellis May has baseball hands.

With that right hand he reaches into the pocket of his shirt, pulls out a bottle cap he brought along for the occasion, and sets it on the table. Bent slightly when it was pried off its bottle, the cap at the crease is lined with rust.

"This is how it all started," he says, pushing the cap across the table. It says "Coke" in loopy, red script letters. It's an old cap, the kind that used to be lined with cork, though that's dried up, shriveled and all but chipped away from the underside of this cap. "I'll never forget, Mr. Jesse Norwood told us, 'Gentlemen,' he said—he always called us 'gentlemen'—'you're going to be as famous as Coke-Cola.'"

"That's right," Madison echoes from behind.

"And we were," May says. "Almost."

"Started in nine-teen fif-ty four," the Candyman says. He settles back in his chair, rubs at his chin a little, summoning the memories. He was the bookkeeper of the team, ultimately, both on the field, and off, compiling statistics, tallying them up for the presentation of year-end awards. So he is the repository of much of the Mohawk folklore. Many of the other players defer to the Candyman for an answer to a question, the fullest version of any particular story.

"He's the talking man," Pugh had said, preferring not to do too much talking himself.

Nineteen fifty-four: These men were boys, ten, eleven, twelve years old; boys who all grew up in the same neighborhood, all lived within a mile of each other. May lists some of the names: Willie Ankum, Robert Brown, Howard Jasper, Bennie Harris, Selma Miles, Leroy Bennett, Theodore Sellers.

"Oh, there must a been fifteen, twenty of us out there in the street, every night, ev-ery night," he says, relishing the memories, adding extra syllables to his words, to make them last longer.

They played corkball out on Bullshead Avenue, every spring evening after school. Corkball, so named because of the corked bottle cap, was the local version of stickball, the street form of baseball played all across the eastern United States, as well as all over Mobile County, not just the back streets of Prichard. In some neighborhoods the families could afford to supply their children with real, store-bought sticks and red rubber Spalding balls, like the ones borough kids bounced off the manhole covers in the paved streets of Brooklyn and Queens. But it was the same game, the same game Frank Bolling says taught him how to stay with a pitch and Hank Aaron credits for his hammering style, attacking the ball. It was the same game Duke Snider could never—not even in the year he hit .341 for the Brooklyn Dodgers, in 1954—master in his summer neighborhood of Bay Ridge. "I couldn't hit the damn thing," Roger Kahn records him as saying. The same game, played everywhere, another of what poet Donald Hall calls the "million apparitions of sticks and crickets and rounders."[7]

There were no teams in the Bullshead version of stickball. There was the pitcher, the batter, and everyone else, twelve, fifteen scrawny black boys still in their school pants, patched, and repatched, ripping new tears, smudging the knees and backsides with the red Alabama clay of the street. They were otherwise stripped down to white sleeveless undershirts and bare feet. The pitcher sidearmed a soda bottle cap, a Coca-Cola cap. It dipped and juked, fluttered like the best of knuckleballs. The batter held a lopped-off broom handle at the ready, high off his back shoulder, wrists loose and poised. Then he swung, a bat no thicker than one of his long bones, his humerus or femur, no bigger than the circumference of a quarter or the quarter-inch-thick bottle cap dancing before him. If he hit it, though only in the air, he could run forward to the one base. If he made it back home before being tagged, he scored a run. Everything else was an out. Three outs and the next batter's up—boys calling out in eager, adolescent voices, "I'm next," or, "Me! *I'm* next!"

They congregated beneath the stout limbs of a mighty oak tree that anchored the corner of Bullshead and Rich Avenues. Randolph's store sat back behind the tree, where they could buy a Coca-Cola, for a nickel, gently pry off the top using the metal claw attached to the front of the big box dispenser, and pass the soda around among the early arrivals. When someone showed up with a broomstick or mop handle, they had a game.

May batted first. He stood over a flattened cereal box used for home plate, windmilling the chipped yellow broomstick in his hands, kicking back his feet like a bull ready to charge, stirring up clouds of fine red dust.

Young Howard Jasper pitched. He leaned over to his right and snaked that arm around, looking like a shiny, black leather bullwhip, before releasing the cap with a snap of his wrist.

The release point made it look to May like the cap would go sailing behind his back, freezing him in his stance as he watched it jitterbug into his wheelhouse, where he could offer only a halfhearted swing.

"I'm next," Ankum called out, after the Candyman wiffed on two more floaters, never making contact.

"Never could hit the deuce," May says.

"Candyman likes the *heat*," Pugh says.

"Dead red," the Candyman admits. Turns out that's the way he likes most everything in life: dead red.

One evening in 1954, Jesse Norwood returned from work, first dropping off Albert Lomax over on Dickerson, then easing the big Buick, one of the few cars in the neighborhood, alongside 1609 Bullshead. Weary from a ten-hour day supervising the Brookley warehouses, Mr. Jesse clomped up the three steps onto the small porch and pulled open the creaking screen door. Inside, he called out to his wife, Hattie, "I'm home, baby," set his lunch pail on the kitchen table, and moved toward the back of the shotgun house, asking after his boys, Melvin and Jesse Jr., their baby sister. He stripped off his soiled uniform top and dropped it into the laundry basket. In the kitchen again he poured himself a glass of tea and then went back out onto the porch and sat on the top step, in his undershirt, relaxing, watching the scrum of boys in the street.

The sun was still high enough in the spring evening sky, the air stagnant and warm. The boys, sweaty and dusty, swarmed after the cap popped up by Harris, converging beneath it, bodies colliding, knocking Ankum to the ground, thin arms stretched over their heads, fingers reaching to make the out.

Almost thirty-six years old at the time, Jesse Norwood had been working since he was not much older than these boys out there in the street before him, whose only concern in life at the moment was the twirling Coke cap falling from the sky. He quit the sixth grade and went to work pulling coal door-to-door in a wooden wagon through the streets of Albany, Georgia, in 1930, after the depression found its way to the Deep South, after his mother followed a railroad man for Mobile in search of work. Jesse had a younger sister, Rose Marie, to support, so he had no time for school, no time for street games. Their father had died some years earlier, from grief, it's said, after their baby brother passed.

"That's a story not many people know," Commissioner Jones says when talking about the impact Uncle Jesse had on his life. He tells the story of the elder Norwood returning to their kerosene-lamp-lighted hut after a full day in the cotton fields, his arms and back aching, his hands all but ruined. Near blind from fatigue, he sat down heavily in the ladder-back chair where his baby boy was napping while the mother cooked up some cornbread on the stove nearby, so injuring the infant that he died. Norwood was inconsolable. He disappeared into the fields surrounding their shack one night and cried himself to death. "Died of grief," Jones says.

The game of corkball ended when the cap was lost in the azalea bushes across Bullshead in the deepening shadows of dusk. The boys searched for a while, never willing to give up the game easily, and then disbanded when no one could produce another nickel.

Two days later Mr. Jesse returned from work with a hard rubber ball he had bought at the Kress Five-and-Dime in downtown Mobile. He gave it to the boys. While that elevated the game, it wasn't long before the impact of the ball snapped off the broom handle in the young boys' hands. Jesse bought them a bat to replace it. By that time, Mr. Jesse had migrated from his perch on the stoop into position to umpire the ragged game. And then, after witnessing another argument over the batting order nearly coming to fisticuffs, Mr. Jesse Norwood stood and called the boys to gather around him.

"Gentlemen," he said, when he had them all assembled, "You want to play baseball?"

They nodded, said, "Yes sir, Mr. Norwood."

"Then let's organize us a team. I'll get some equipment, find us a place to play. You boys meet me over there," he said, pointing toward the small porch at the front of number 1609. "All right?"

"Yes sir," May says. "That's how it started."

Pugh pushes himself into a more upright position in his chair, stretches out his left hand, points, and says, "I thought you said it started with that soda cap."

Others, Madison, Emanuel, chuckle softly.

"Mr. Secretary," Candyman says to Emanuel without turning around, "make a note that Lyonel is fined five dollars for his in-subordination."

"Oh, Sweet," Madison says, pulling down on the

brim of his hat. "Why you want to do that?"

Pugh just throws up his large hands in surrender, slouches back in his chair.

Their first playing field was a vacant lot four doors down from the Norwood homestead, next to Emanuel's. Norwood arrived home to find the boys milling about his front yard, wrestling, playing tag. They walked down the street to the lot and cleared it of rocks, broken glass, stray timber. They stretched chicken coop wire across the back end of the lot facing busy St. Stephens Road for a backstop. Jesse bought a set of bases, more bats, real baseballs, and enough gloves to get started. Their initial games, played on Sunday afternoon after the churches let out, were intrasquad matchups of six against six, half a dozen players more than enough to defensively cover the 40-by-150-foot lot. Then more boys showed up, and along with them, spectators, something that surprised the boys, even scared them a little. Neighbors and mothers, still in their church finery, their hats and costume jewelry, dragged kitchen chairs and stools out into the street to watch the nascent games.

One weeknight after practice Mr. Jesse spoke to the players gathered back at 1609 Bullshead for water and iced tea. "Gentlemen, we need us a name," he said. They needed a name those mothers and neighbors and other spectators could associate with, even whisper throughout the other neighborhoods of

Prichard and Mobile. At a time when people still sat out on their porches of a spring or summer evening, exchanging pleasantries with passersby, when they still walked to work, or to the store, to school or church, they needed a name that could be passed along that network as easily as comments about the weather or reports of a relative's health or the birth of a new baby.

The boys bandied about some possibilities, mostly variations on names of the other teams they knew about in the area, the Prichard Athletics, the Blue Devils, the Hillsdale Cardinals. Until May piped up and said, "We're playing on Bullshead. Why don't we call ourselves the Bullshead *Giants*."

It may have been that moment when Jesse Norwood recognized the true utility Ellis May possessed, that he would become the spokesman of the team, that even as a young boy he could speak to the figurative purpose of the whole endeavor, he could pronounce these boys *giants*. It was then that Jesse set the democratic tone that would shape the organization throughout the next decade and a half. "It's your team," he told them. "What do y'all think?"

"We became the Giants," May says.

"The Giants?" Emanuel asks. "When was that?"

"In the beginning," Candyman tells him. "In the beginning."

Emanuel, like Pugh and Madison, actually came

to the team later, after they changed the name. Even though he lived in the neighborhood, he was playing for his father on the Paradise Park Cubs, along with Pugh, who grew up "on the *other* side of the tracks," he says, and chuckles.

Mr. Jesse convinced the elder Emanuel, his neighbor and friend, to join him that first summer. And when he did, young Emanuel followed, of his own choice, as did Pugh, after several years with the Cubs. Those two recruited Madison from the Blue Devils a year later.

"That's right," Sam says.

May raises his hands and says, "We're getting ahead of ourselves, gentlemen." As close as he is to these men, as much as they all openly express their love for one another, May doesn't really want to talk about the recruitment of Pugh, and then Madison. Not yet. The room quiets again. "Let's go back to the beginning," he says.

The Giants overran their space on Bullshead in a matter of weeks, with the burgeoning Sunday crowds and the advancement of their baseball skills, hitting balls onto neighboring property, even breaking a window or two. Mr. Jesse found available land across St. Stephens behind the Lincoln Funeral Home on Victor Avenue, an open field on a tract of land known as Dozier's Alley. Here, the boys had to pull grass clumps and rake smooth the dirt and red clay, mix in sand poured from hundred-pound bags, where the bases, a pitcher's mound, home plate, and batter's boxes would go. They hacked away at the perimeter woods, sculpting an outfield nearly symmetrical in its dimensions. They pounded four-by-four posts into the ground behind home, strung more chicken wire for the backstop.

The field, accessible only after a lengthy walk across St. Stephens, through the surrounding woods, wasn't exactly level. Rainwater from frequent summer thunderstorms would flood the infield of the low-lying parcel, but that wouldn't stop the baseball. They layered gasoline over the wet grass and dirt, burned off the moisture. Play ball.

The boys worked their park, practiced their skills every day during the week, and played their simulated Sunday games, with enough players now to field full lineups against each other. And still, the fans came. They trekked across St. Stephens, through the woods, carrying chairs, sacks of fried chicken and biscuits, to watch their boys play.

The earliest games at Dozier's were often just a series of drills Mr. Jesse would guide them through as he came to understand more and more about baseball. They weren't playing against visiting opponents just yet.

"Let's do that again," he'd call out from his seat on a church pew behind the wiring that served as a dugout. On a line drive hit to right-center field, with a runner on first, he noticed some of his fielders hadn't rotated correctly.

"You got to be in the right place, gentlemen."

Emanuel Senior came in from his third base coach's position and took up the bat. He hit another rope into the outfield, with Mr. Jesse calling out to his players in his raspy voice, "Who covers second?" He asked, "What about the cutoff?" He moved the boys around like chess pieces. "Everybody's got a job," Mr. Jesse called out over the field. "Everybody's got a job."

He instructed Selma Miles to come down the left field line to back up Ellis should the throw come to third, "in case we got a rabbit on the bases running with the pitch," he explained.

Jesse then walked up the first base line, motioning Brown, the runner, over, telling him to do just that, calling out, "Go," as soon as the ball was tossed into the air. Emanuel stroked it toward the outfield. Leroy Bennett charged over from center, scooping up the ball as Brown was rounding second. The players rotated. Jesse told his catcher, George Ankum, to call the throw.

"Third base!"

Brown was out by five paces.

"Howard," Coach Norwood called to Brooks in right, who hadn't moved much, "What if that ball gets by Leroy?"

"I've got to back him up, Mr. Norwood," the answer came. Howard nodding understanding, rehearsing his steps, trotted to his right to show it.

"That's right," Jesse said, returning behind the screen, repeating, "*Everybody's* got a job," taking up his seat on the pew once again. "Let's play ball."

"Everybody's got a job," May says.

"You just got to be in the right place," Madison adds, these men freely repeating the maxims called out to them over and over throughout the hours upon hours spent on the ball field. There's a wistfulness that creeps into their voices from time to time, a sense that even with the memories of Mr. Jesse's method, and his messages, even the approximate *sound* of his voice, which many of them can believably replicate, it's the man they miss, who they wish, thirty-some years after his death, could be in that room with them, could witness this moment.

To the parents and neighbors and friends watching those drills, sitting in their chairs, fanning themselves against the Alabama summer heat with postcards or change purses, porkpie hats, anything, they could see the team, their preteen boys, most of them still awkward in their adolescence, arms and legs akimbo when they tried to move through the scripted paces, gel into a cohesive and unified unit right before their eyes.

The pews, two each set up along either flank of home plate, had come from an old church recently torn down. Mr. Jesse bought the pews and all the salvageable timber from the wood-frame building for a hundred dollars. With the planking, he built a clubhouse for the team behind his residence at 1609 Bullshead. Here the boys came every Saturday night for team meetings, to discuss the week's progress, the next day's lineups, their assignments for the coming week. They studied baseball and more. The hour-long meetings were, the Candyman says, "fifteen minutes of baseball and forty-five minutes of life."

Jesse Norwood, with less than a sixth-grade education, who'd never played organized sports himself, learned what he did of baseball, and most everything else, from books. And he imparted both his knowledge and his methodology to his team. He encouraged the boys to read and study, prodding their young minds even as he was molding their baseball skills, changing their lives. He was a second father to some, and the only father figure in the lives of many of them, including Ellis May.

"He was the only father I ever knew," Candyman says. His father had left when Ellis was still a baby. His mother worked as a domestic in Mobile. The only pair of shoes Ellis owned before he became a Mohawk was cast off from the white family his mother worked for, the soles wired on, with cardboard lasts. "The only father."

Madison puts it more directly: "I wouldn't be alive today if not for Mr. Jesse Norwood."

Then Emanuel ups the ante some more. "Jesse

Norwood was God." A man of the cloth himself, Emanuel doesn't make such statements lightly.

There's an awkward silence in the room, until Candyman says, "Dead red, Reverend Emanuel, dead red," which brings a smile to their faces and breaks the trance.

May turns around in his seat and reaches to clasp Emanuel's hand. "But first," he says, steering the discussion back to baseball, "we changed the name of the team."

From a book first published in 1851, called *League of the Ho-de-no-sau-nee, or Iroquois*, Mr. Jesse learned about the Mohawks. He was first struck by the loose translation of the name *Iroquois*, "people of the longhouse," which, from the pictures, looked a lot like one of the shotgun houses along Bullshead Avenue and throughout Prichard. He learned that the longhouses were ceremonial buildings as well as communal dwellings, that the Mohawks, already a sovereign people for several hundred years, taught the earliest European settlers how to survive America's northern climate. He learned that, as one of the six nations of the Iroquois Confederacy, the Mohawks practiced one of the world's first true democracies, that Thomas Jefferson studied the values and beliefs of the Iroquois, and it was their political system that became the model for the original thirteen colonies.

It was the same model Jesse Norwood employed one Saturday evening in the summer of 1954 when he suggested the name change and offered it to the floor of their clubhouse for a vote. The decision was unanimous, and the former Bullshead Giants became the Prichard Mohawks.

Two

*I*f 1954 was the beginning, the *foundation* of the Mohawks, then that single day in March of 1948 when Brooklyn came to Mobile was one of the earliest cornerstones of that foundation, just as it was one of the earliest stepping stones on the path to racial equality for the rest of the country. Jackie Robinson was the trailblazer of that path, sure-footed and strident, confident in his abilities, defying the stereotypes and assumptions, replacing the utter despair that otherwise engulfed most other Negroes in America, young men especially, with promise and potential. In the eighty years since the devastating internal conflict fought over abolition and emancipation, there were still two Americas; there was still a civil war raging, even if the battle was being waged over such pedestrian issues as *civility* itself, basic human decency, rather than open hostilities fighting for freedom and secession. "One ever feels his twoness," W. E. B. DuBois wrote in 1903, "an American, a Negro; two souls, two thoughts, two unreconciled strivings; two warring ideals in one dark body."[8]

Jackie Robinson, over the course of his first season in the majors in 1947, had brought those worlds together.

The Dodgers were fresh off the thrilling 1947 World Series, where they'd taken the Yankees to a game seven before submitting. Leo Durocher, who'd started the year, if not the season, at the helm of the Dodgers, who might have been the ingredient that could have wrested the championship away from the New Yorkers DiMaggio, Heinrich, Rizzuto, Berra, Allie Reynolds, and Spec Shea, was back with the team after his suspension a year earlier by commissioner A. B. "Happy" Chandler for consorting with unsavory types, gamblers, specifically.[9]

The rest of the ingredients, most of the pennant-winning talent of 1947, were still with the team, including the Rookie of the Year, Jackie Robinson. That Yankee team, by comparison, hardly lived up to their reputation as the "Bronx Bombers." DiMaggio, the leading hitter on the team, batted a less-than-robust .315. His twenty home runs also led the team. The next leading hitter was George Mcquinn, at .305. Heinrich finished second in homers with sixteen. No one on the team drove in as many as a hundred runs. "Comparatively speaking, these were peashooters, not bombers."[10]

They got by on defense and the pitching of Reynolds and Shea, Joe Page and Spud Chandler. The essential difference at the end of the 1947 season, what separated the Yankees from the Dodgers, was management, according to most.

Red Barber, in his memoir published in 1954, called the 1947 World Series "the greatest Series ever played." Writing at the time for the *Herald Tribune*, Al Laney said the Series "provided perhaps more thrills and more hysteria than any other." Though it was televised, the medium was in its infancy and quite unreliable, even if you owned one of those early sets made by Admiral or DuMont. It was still very much a live event, without videotape, without replay, though there was plenty of second-guessing, especially of the decisions made by then-Dodger-manager Burt Shotton. His twenty-one-year-old ace, Ralph Branca, started game one and pitched four perfect innings before getting rattled in the fifth. Yankee manager Bucky Harris outmanaged Shotton, capitalizing on Branca's difficulties, and stole the game. Worse, and unaccountably, Branca, who'd had the year of his life, did not start another game in the series. Other questionable decisions followed, and in the decisive game seven, Shotton benched Al Gionfriddo, a day after he'd made what DiMaggio would always consider one of the greatest catches ever, of a quality to rival even Mays's epic grab of Vic Wertz's drive in 1954.

But even with Durocher back in the dugout, all was not well with the club picked to again become National League champs and perhaps capture baseball's ultimate prize, a World Series ring, even before

they arrived for spring training in what was then
called Ciudad Trujillo, in the Dominican Republic, in
February of 1948.

Two years earlier, in February of 1946, on his way
to his first spring training with the Dodger organization, Jackie and Rachel Robinson had been forced off
a plane in Pensacola, Florida. They were told the
plane needed additional fuel for passage through a
storm brewing along the Gulf. The need turned out to
be two white passengers receiving preferential treatment. The Robinsons had to then ride a bus the
remainder of the way, relegated to the back, of course.
Once there, the Montreal players were whisked from
their usual training site to that of the parent club, the
Dodger facilities in Daytona Beach, because of threats
of violence over banned interracial competition.
Branch Rickey subsequently moved the teams to
Havana, Cuba, after an armed sheriff had interrupted
an exhibition game between Brooklyn and their Montreal affiliate, announcing that "nigras" didn't mix
with whites in his jurisdiction, "Now git," he said,
brandishing his pistol. Jackie was forced to leave the
field. He almost left the team, and baseball, entirely.
Wendell Smith, traveling with Jackie that first spring,
had to convince Jackie to stay in uniform, that things
would get better. While accommodations in Cuba were
still segregated, the situation was not life-threatening.

In Montreal, living and playing the 1946 season
for the team housed safely across the northern border

of the racially divided United States, Robinson was so dominant and so popular that a pack of adoring fans eager to show their appreciation after a particularly crucial game chased him through the streets of Montreal. Jackie ran for his life as if from a lynch mob in south Florida or the Mississippi Delta.

Bypassing Florida for Cuba altogether prior to the 1947 season, the team avoided only external racial problems. When it became obvious during spring training that Rickey intended to integrate the Dodgers, some of the white players objected so vehemently they circulated a petition gathering the signatures of those who intended to boycott play if Robinson was promoted. Durocher stymied the insurrection in a manner typical of his style, only weeks before his suspension. He directed his coaches to assemble the players in the middle of the night once he caught wind of the movement. With his team of professional ball players gathered around in their nightclothes and underwear, Leo the Lip addressed them. "You know what you can use that petition for," he said to the bleary, yawning men. "You can wipe your ass."

Now that they were awake, he continued, "I'm the manager and I'm paid to win and I'd play an elephant if he could win for me and this fellow Robinson is no elephant. You can't throw him out on the bases and you can't get him out at the plate. This fellow is a great player. He's gonna win pennants. He's gonna put money in your pockets and mine."[11]

In 1947, even without their fiery manager, the Dodgers did just that, in large part due to the presence of Jackie Robinson.

But Robinson showed up for spring training in Ciudad Trujillo in 1948 twenty-five pounds over-weight. He'd spent the off-season on the lecture cir-cuit, speaking at churches, community centers, schools, bringing his message of hope and opportu-nity, testifying to the fact that what might have seemed impossible only a year earlier was now pos-sible. The living, breathing, flesh-and-blood Jackie Robinson meant that it was possible. Whatever their dream was, it was now possible, within reach. It had taken bloodletting and bruised flesh, he said, but that was a small price to pay. In the end, he'd won respect from his peers and adoration from the game's scribes. He'd proved that baseball's "noble experiment" was workable.

"The integration of baseball," historian Jules Tygiel wrote, "represented both a symbol of imminent racial challenge and a direct agent of social change. Jackie Robinson's campaign against the color line in 1946-47 captured the imagination of millions of Americans who had previously ignored the nation's racial dilemma."[12]

What the citizens and schoolchildren of those black communities brought to thank Jackie for his message was food. And Robinson loved to eat, especially the rich home-cooked meals brimming with sugars and starches brought from the impoverished kitchens of those audiences so appreciative of the message he brought to their towns—the fried chicken and squash casseroles, the barbecued pork and potato salad, sweet tea and bread pudding. Roger Kahn reported, "His attack on a wedge of apple pie, topped with two scoops of vanilla ice cream, was an exercise in passion. His discipline had been saintly across the season of 1947. After the World Series, it collapsed."[13]

Branch Rickey was so disappointed that he placed Robinson on waivers. Any of the other teams could have claimed him for ten thousand dollars. None did.

Durocher was enraged. "That colored son of a bitch stayed in shape for Shotton"—Burt Shotton, the man who'd replaced Durocher a year earlier—"who meant nothing. I'm the guy who knocked down the petition. I'm the guy who fought for Robinson. And when he shows up to play for me, he looks like a black tub of lard."[14]

Durocher fed his overweight star a steady diet of infield drills each day, making him wear an upper-body rubber suit in the 90-degree tropical heat, blistering ground balls to his left and right. Jackie had to scamper one way, then another, ranging farther than an infielder normally would, bend, reach, and scoop up the ball, firing it back into home. Every day, until he was nearly exhausted, until Durocher would announce, in front of the sportswriters covering the team, the other players, the rookie prospects trying to earn a position, in front of adoring fans who'd turned out to watch, "Stick a fork in him, boys. He's done." By the time they broke camp in the Caribbean, Robinson had lost fifteen pounds, but manager and star weren't speaking.

Jackie knew it was wrong of him to report so out of shape, but he thought it just as wrong for Durocher to humiliate him like that. "To tell the truth," Jackie said before it was all over, "I hated the loudmouthed bastard."[15]

That was the state of things when the team rolled into Mobile. In that mood, Robinson might have considered the honing effect of the hard-packed, rust-colored Alabama clay of Hartwell Field's base paths, infield, and batter's box on the metal spikes of his baseball shoes as he trotted around the horn for warm-ups and took batting practice. Much of the reported saintly discipline of the year before had been restraint, Jackie's not responding to the onslaught of abuse he suffered throughout the season. Runners barreling down the first base line trying to leg out an infield ground ball had viciously spiked whichever foot Robinson had planted on the bag, awaiting the throw from a teammate. Opposing players and coaches and fans hurled all manner of invective and insult and slur at him upon his every move on the road. He was gouged, beaned, and spat on; he had his life threatened, with specific enough threats at times that the FBI attended Dodgers' games. But he endured it all with restraint, even equanimity, for a greater purpose: Rickey's "noble experiment." Jackie maintained his dignity, as promised, as part of Rickey's three-year plan toward establishing the integration of baseball.

"Do you want someone who would not have the courage to fight back?" Jackie is said to have asked during that famous exchange.

A deeply religious man, who wouldn't take the field as a player or manager on the Sabbath, Rickey read to Robinson from Papini's *Life of Christ*, the model of personal sacrifice for a greater purpose. Turn the other cheek, was the message. Rickey considered the endeavor that important, always had.

"I want you to have the courage *not* to fight back," he thundered in response, an example of Gandhian nonviolent resistance as the strategy toward combating racially motivated abuse.

That didn't mean, though, that Robinson couldn't respond in whatever way was permissible within the confines of the game, charging into catchers guarding the plate or applying breath-robbing tags to runners. And if he considered the flint quality of the Hartwell surface, putting the slightest of edges on those gleaming metal spikes, he couldn't have been blamed, though there were no altercations that day, none that anyone has been recorded noticing. Most of the fans spread around the old wooden bleachers noticed little more than the dark tones of his skin, what would be described before he was done as "imperial ebony," set against his gray flannel uniform, a stark contrast to most of the rest of the Dodgers, and certainly all of the Mobile team. To the white fans, it was still an oddity, seeing a black man playing on the same field as the rest, though not a completely unfamiliar spectacle. To the black contingent, though, relegated to the right field bleachers, the sight of Jackie Robinson, big-league Jackie Robinson, was a vision of promise, a harbinger of better things to come.

Between those views, there was baseball, a cordial, incomplete exhibition game that allowed everyone on either side of the contest a chance to participate. The game was lazy and lighthearted, little more than an excuse to get out and frolic beneath the bright sunshine and Gulf breezes of a coastal Alabama spring day. Pitchers served up batting-practice-type tosses, allowing power hitters like Duke Snider of the Dodgers and Connors of Mobile, television's "Rifleman" of the 1960s, to strut their stuff, the crowd oohing and aahing at each ball lofted toward the fences festooned with local advertising for Sunbeam Bread, Dixie Crystal Sugar, and Wagner Plumbing. It was as if they were witnessing a fireworks display down along the waterfront. The only likely violence that day would have been another broken window in the Mobile Pulley and Machine Works factory on Tennessee Street, just beyond the right field fence. There was no aggressive base running, no taunting, and no managerial maneuvering. Rounding first base languidly after his own high fly ball to center field, turning and trotting back across the infield after the ball was caught by Shuba, his former and future teammate, heading for the dugout, Robinson may have experienced some vestigial sense of his birthplace back in Cairo, Georgia, just a hundred and fifty miles to the northeast. The air was thick with Gulf moisture, a hint of salt and fish. The scent of honeysuckle hung suspended there. Or perhaps the entire atmosphere in the park, where there was very little animosity on the field, a palpable tolerance in the stands, freed Jackie to relax from the determined vigilance he'd had to employ throughout every inning of every game the year before. He was allowed, for that day at least, to just enjoy playing the game again.

While there may have been militant resistance to the appearance of Robinson's Dodgers in other southern cities, other Alabama venues, Mobile was relatively much more progressive. That has been attributed to several factors, baseball being a prominent example. But the population mix of Mobile, a city to which people flocked from all parts of the South during the war for work down on the burgeoning docks, was also more varied and dynamic than other staid and depressed communities clinging to the old order. And Mobile benefited from the early liberal political attitude of Joe Langham, a white city councilman who'd protested the segregated public transportation system in the city years before the Montgomery bus boycott. Quite probably no one really noticed Robinson's extra ten pounds, or that he was not yet able to make that first explosive step on his way to another stolen base, not as quick to get down the line to beat out a bunt or stretch a routine ground ball into an infield single. Not yet, but almost.

There was one man in the crowd of thousands who might have realized the absence of Robinson's customary lean, lightning agility and speed.

But then James Harris says he was watching with a more critical eye than most. Harris, like a handful of other players from Mobile plying the old Negro Southern League circuit, felt, at the time, that if he'd been in a different place, maybe, in a slightly different era, it could have been him out there in that Brooklyn uniform. More than forty-five years later, it's a wistful thought, a bittersweet memory. No more than that.

"Don't get me wrong," he says. "When Jackie made it, it was the greatest thing that could have happened. You wouldn't *believe* how much your chest can swell up overnight, at the thought, just the thought that you could have been Jackie Robinson."

He sits slouched against a stack of pillows on an

overstuffed couch in the den of his tidy brick home in south Mobile County. He's wearing an "Elect Sam Jones" T-shirt and yellow Bermuda shorts. Red-striped tube socks cover most of the rest of his stumpy legs. There's a white hand towel draped over his left shoulder, to dab at the sweat that will bead up on his forehead when he mows the postage-stamp-size lawn around the house later in the afternoon. Harris will rinse the towel in cold water from the outside spigot and drape it around his neck, cooling his blood as he continues the task, slowly, on aching, unsteady legs.

He pushes himself up straighter with his stout forearms, leans forward, cocks his head, squints, and says, "We *knew* we could play."

Already past his thirtieth birthday when Robinson was signed by Rickey's scouts, Harris wouldn't have been given a second glance. They were looking for younger phenoms, men with steely tempers as well as explosive skills. "Still," Harris repeats, "we knew we could play."

Harris had, in fact, in his role of baseball godfather, helped arrange a tryout for two Mobile players, Terris "Speed" McDuffie and Dave "Showboat" Thomas, with Rickey and the Dodgers in 1945, six months before they signed Jackie Robinson.

Harris was more of a contemporary of Satchel Paige, who would make it to the major leagues with Cleveland that year of 1948; though in his forties, he was that good. "He was the best," Harris says. Dizzy

Dean once said that his own supposedly dizzying fastball looked like a change of pace compared to the little bullets Paige threw across the plate, what Paige called his "Stinger."

"You know how he was all the time boasting he was going to strike out the first nine hitters he faced, telling his fielders to sit down and take a rest? I seen him do it," Harris adds, chuckling. "But," he raises a finger. "I took him *down-town* once," he says, savoring the words, the memory. "Yup. I rang one off the big man, and there's not a lot of people in the whole *world* that can say that!"

Harris shifts his position on the couch, rearranges the pillows trying to find the right compression point to ease his aching back, long enough to finish a sentence anyway, or another story. "Too many years behind the dish," he says of his ailment.

Harris was a catcher for the old Mobile Black Shippers, one of a series of corresponding black contingents to Mobile's white minor league teams. On the surface, the practice was an obvious adherence to the requirements of the Jim Crow South, but in actuality, the teams were never completely separate, nor were they, to hear Harris tell it, anything like equal. The white teams and black teams played each other regularly, he says. "And we whooped 'em, every time." He says they whooped nearly everyone they played, even the greatest American and National Negro League teams when they barnstormed through. "Whooped 'em good," he says.

It's hard to tell if Harris is relating anything like verifiable fact or merely offering up a taste of that other compendium of baseball history, its folklore. It doesn't really matter, of course, least of all to him. He volunteers no apologies. Instead, he tells the story of an encounter with the great Josh Gibson, the colored Babe Ruth, who had been considered early on as a candidate to shoulder black baseball's mantle across the color line, before he died in 1947. Aaron Watson just rolls his eyes when recalling Gibson's talent. "You know he died of grief," he says, from being passed over by Rickey. Gibson was a superlative catcher himself and a prodigious home run hitter. The duo of Gibson and Paige on the Pittsburgh Crawfords is considered by some to be the greatest battery the game has ever seen.

"Struck him out," Harris says of a time when his Black Bears played the Crawfords down at Hartwell. "Struck him out with the game on the line"—by which he means he'd coaxed a young knuckleballer through the necessary paces to get the out. "We threw five straight floaters at him. He watched the first one, just to gauge it. I could see him measuring the thing. And it slipped by for a strike. He stood there pumping that big stick he used, ready. Showed him another knuckler that he just missed. We wasted the next pitch, and the next one, and the next one—knucklers, every one of them, so he's thinking that's all we got." Harris pushes himself off the couch and stands there in the dim morning light, taking up a batter's stance, crouched over, waving an imaginary bat in his hands. "Three and two. I could see him sneaking a peek back at me, trying to see if I was going to call some other pitch. I shrugged, made sure he saw me. He got all excited, urging me to bring it on, 'Bring it on!' We crossed him up with a fastball that he was so far behind it should have counted as *two* strikes. Game over. We win," he says, and chuckles, then repeats, "We *knew* we could play," sitting back down in obvious pain but with a most satisfied look on his face.

After several moments of trying to find a comfortable position, he says, "I used to think that anyone who wants to play catcher ought to be put in a straitjacket. But then, when I got older, I figured it's the only position to play, to *really* learn the game. And I loved the game, loved it ever since I can remember." He tells a story of seeing Babe Ruth play out at Monroe Park once, as a little boy in the twenties. "He hit a home run so hard it looked like a rocket taking off. Course we didn't know nothing about rockets at the time. We just stared after that thing soaring through the sky. We didn't know what it was. It cleared that stadium and flew all the way to the rail yard and into a moving freight train. I don't think it *ever* stopped traveling," he says, closing his eyes and shaking his head.

"Man, I loved that game. Still love it. Still play, every night," he says, opening his eyes again, waiting.

"E-very night. I'm running the bases, chasing down foul pop-ups; gets so I can't hardly get down the stairs in the morning." Harris starts to laughing so hard he chokes and has to take a minute to settle himself down.

Harris played through his forties, but as a player-coach and manager, with local teams. The only traveling he did was as a talent scout. He managed out at Mitchell Field in Prichard. It was there that young Henry Aaron came under his tutelage. Aaron was formerly known as a softball star in the area, until he heard Jackie Robinson's talk after his exhibition game in Mobile in the spring of 1948.

"I was only fourteen years old," Aaron says in a *Time* magazine article. "Jackie spoke to a big crowd of black folks over on Davis Avenue. I think he talked about segregation, but I didn't hear a word that came out of his mouth. Jackie Robinson was such a hero to me that I couldn't do anything but gawk."

Aaron already knew all about segregation. In 1948, life was segregation, two worlds afraid of each other. There were segregated schools and restaurants, whites-only and colored-only water fountains. And for the most part, life was unkind to any black man who tried to bring those worlds together. Then along came Jackie Robinson. "God bless him," Aaron says. "He was bigger than that life."[16]

It was at Mitchell Field where Harris also coached Billy Williams, who went on to the Chicago Cubs and became nearly as popular there as Ernie Banks, Mr. Cub. What Harris remembers of Billy is that he had older brothers who were just as talented. "*Two* of them," Harris says, holding up the requisite fingers. "Oh, we had some talent in this town. Nobody hardly knew it, but we had us some talent."

Harris talks about timing again, wondering out loud why it took so long for anyone to notice the baseball being played in Mobile. It's an indigestible irony for him, that there was the Bears, a Brooklyn farm club, yet it took so long for any Dodger scouts to venture out to Mitchell Field or Prichard Stadium to witness the *real* baseball talent in Mobile. He could have told them, if only they'd asked.

Eventually, they would ask. "It's a timing thing," he says, "like hitting a baseball." They still ask. He's still called upon, into his seventies, to render his assessment of young regional baseball prospects. "And I do it too," he says. "But I don't like to travel so much anymore."

It was as a traveling scout for the San Francisco Giants that Harris brought Willie McCovey to a tryout in Jasmine, Mississippi. Another Mobilian, Bill Dillard, was on that same trip.

"Nineteen fifty-seven was the year," Dillard says, the year Harris took him, Ralph Taylor, and Willie McCovey across the state line to Jasmine for the tryout. He'd been playing for Harris for three years, playing for a traveling professional team while he was still in high school. "We got five dollars a game when we went out of state," he says with evident glee at what a staggering amount of money that was for him, considering the times. But because Dillard was a minor on that team of adults, he couldn't be paid directly. Harris held the money for him until he graduated. He was good enough, though, to warrant such special treatment.

Attending the same tryout as those three teenaged black players were about thirty-five white ballplayers from the region. But Dillard and Taylor and McCovey didn't work out against the white players. They didn't even try out the same day on the same field. Their tryout was the next day, after the scouts and coaches had seen all the other talent, on a field in the other part of town.

Dillard sits in a booth by the window of the McDonald's in downtown Mobile on Government Street. He cradles his cup of coffee in both hands, like it's an egg, as an infielder would. "Everyone *knew* they were only going to sign one of us, if they signed any at all. Me, I could catch most anything I could get to, and knock down a lot of other stuff. I played a busy third base," he says, crouching even now, in his seat. "And Taylor could throw hard, real hard. But you should have seen Stretch swat that ball. He had those long arms and legs so that they couldn't get anything

by him. And by the time he finished uncoiling everything, like a clock bust open, that ball would be out of
the park, into the woods, Mr. Green hollering, 'Find
me that ball!' to all the little kids that'd come out to
watch. And Willie stood there at the plate for the
longest time just a-swatting and grinning at those
boys scurrying around out there. You should have
seen him."

They signed Willie McCovey that day. "It was a
September day, a fall day. You could feel the greatness,"
he says.

Dillard was just a kid when Jackie Robinson came
to Mobile. But to hear Harris tell it, he became talented enough, fast enough, good enough with his bat,
better with the glove, to have been in the major
leagues, except for the timing involved, and the color
of his skin, even as late as thirteen, fourteen years
after Jackie's breakthrough. He was, in the vernacular
of the day, the colored Brooks Robinson, the great Baltimore Oriole third baseman, a defensive vacuum
cleaner, they said.

"We had us some players down here," Harris says
sadly. He would continue to mold those players
through the decades, trek them all over the southeast
to get them noticed and signed. Dillard, after a couple
such near misses with destiny, would resign himself to
playing in the semipro leagues around Mobile, would
become, in time, a Prichard Mohawk. And it is those
times, the time he spent playing for Jesse Norwood,

that he remembers most fondly.

"Once I started playing for Mr. Jesse," he says, finishing his coffee. "I didn't *want* to go anywhere else."

Dillard says this as if he's been challenged by the claim in the past, questioned, You wouldn't, really— would you?—turn down a chance to play for a major league club and stay in Prichard, with the Mohawks?

He says again, "I didn't *want* to go anywhere else," like it's the most obvious sentiment there could be. And perhaps it is, for him.

One of the more insidious aspects of segregation was the prejudice blacks suffered from, a demeaning assumption of inferiority held over their heads that they were forever forced to dispel, something impossible to fully appreciate unless you lived it, like Dillard did. For him, and a lot of other very, very good baseball players in Mobile and elsewhere, it meant treading a fine line between absolute dismissal and damnation, or artificial comparison, however favorable, neither of which was fair, or humane, or anything like authentic *integration*.

James Baldwin, in a letter to his nephew, his namesake, marking the hundredth anniversary of emancipation, wrote, "Please try to be clear, dear James, through the storm that rages about your youthful head today, about the reality which lies behind the words *acceptance* and *integration*. There is no reason for you to try to become like white people and there is no basis whatever for their impertinent

assumption that *they* must accept *you*. The really terrible thing, old buddy, is that *you* must accept *them*…
You must accept them and accept them with love."[17]

He goes on to tell young James, fourteen at the time, born very near the time Robinson made his appearance in Mobile, "if the word *integration* means anything, this is what it means: that we, with love, shall force our brothers to see themselves as they really are, to cease fleeing from reality and start to change it."[18]

That was the task, which was also a handicap, for all but the strongest of characters, like Jackie Robinson. For men of lesser resolve, or patience, or tolerance, a Bill Dillard, even a Josh Gibson, who suffered from both the practice of segregation *and* from being compared to and measured against Babe Ruth, it was a burden too heavy to bear. Why wouldn't they, the question must be asked, choose to stay where they were appreciated, and accepted, for who they were, however ignominious?

"That's what was so important about Jackie Robinson's success," Harris says. "Not that he was *chosen*. Lord, we knew that was going to happen. That was just a matter of timing. We *knew* we could play," he says one last time, the meaning behind the emphatic repetition clearer now. "He played on his terms. He acknowledged the conditions and then forced acceptance on *his* terms. You didn't hear

anyone saying he was the colored Ty Cobb or anything like that. No sir, he was Jackie Robinson."

Robinson's famous temperament, his insistence
on being treated as an individual person, a human
being, in any context, is evident all throughout his
baseball career and his life. In Pasadena, where his
mother relocated the family while Jackie was still just
an infant, he attended integrated schools, he played
on white teams in high school and college, he was an
officer in the military. He *knew* black men could be
leaders in a white man's world, and that knowledge
fueled a temper that often landed him in trouble with
authorities. One writer has said, "That a man with
such a hair-trigger temper could have survived the
restrictions imposed on him in that breakthrough
major league season seems all the more remarkable."[19]

Such an intrepid constitution is impossible to
measure by any athletic standard, something not even
Branch Rickey, with all of his supposed insight, could
have gauged. Because of it, Jackie Robinson was perfectly destined to break down baseball's and America's
color barrier, whether that ultimately happened
through willful determination or providence. Where
it came from is worth considering, and David Falkner,
in his *Great Time Coming*, offers this clue:

"What is missing in the Jackie Robinson story as
it has been handed down is the period in his life when
the principal effect of his mother's teaching was not

that the future would work out, but that it would not."

He had to, Jackie's mother was saying, put his faith in God. That was just about the very best stance any black person could assume, prior to 1947, when Jackie crossed the color line, "the problem," DuBois said, "of the twentieth century."[20]

And that is why Jackie's promotion to the Dodgers, his appearance in Mobile that day in 1948, his whole career, was so great, "the greatest thing that could have happened," as Harris says, without any real trace of envy. Because he knows—just as Martin Luther King Jr. stressed, "You will never know how easy it was for me because of Jackie Robinson,"[21] — how probable it is that only Jack Roosevelt Robinson could have accomplished what he did, both as a man and as a player.

Three

*L*eading the caravan headed west-northwest out of Mobile County, Alabama, Jesse Norwood's 1956 blue Chevrolet station wagon labored with a capacity load of scrawny, angular boys in brand-new baseball uniforms and their equipment. Along with the bats and helmets and gloves, there was extra water should the radiator boil over, extra hoses should any burst, and two spare tires. This was the first season the Prichard Mohawks were taking to the road and Mr. Jesse wanted to be prepared for anything. This was their first real test, in many ways. Behind him an older sedan sagged under the weight of more boys, more equipment jammed into its trunk. And behind them were mothers and fathers and aunts and uncles, residents of Prichard, Alabama, following the team.

The two lead cars were so burdened their rear ends scraped against the crowned asphalt rise of some of the intersections along the route, spitting up plumes of bright orange sparks, as if the road were a foundry stone forging well-wrought men out of these rough hewn boys. Mr. Jesse, with the hoses and the water and the tires, and anything else he could give them or teach them, was determined to see they completed their trip.

It was the spring of 1957, the spring after Jackie Robinson retired. Earlier in the year federal marshals had gone into Little Rock, Arkansas, and enforced the edict of *Brown v. the Board of Education of Topeka, Kansas*. There were still only forty-eight states in 1957. Sputnik I would launch the space age that fall, and it was the last year the Dodgers would call Brooklyn home, with Walter O'Malley uprooting the franchise to move it to Los Angeles. It was also the year Hank Aaron won the National League Most Valuable Player Award and his Braves won the World Series.

Some of the boys chattered, like so many blackbirds in the cornrows that surrounded their home field back in Prichard. Ellis May, for one, talked about baseball, and girls, and the cars he was going to drive, the money he was going to make. Ellis talked all the time, especially now that his voice had changed into a syrupy, seductive tenor. Others, like Willie Lomax and Bennie Harris, said little, if anything. When the chatter grew too loud, the boys too boisterous, Mr. Jesse glanced up to the rearview mirror, said, "Gentlemen," and they quieted down again, but not for long. He didn't want to dampen their excitement, just temper it some.

Only the beginning of April, it was already hot down in southern Alabama, and stuffy in the car. The woolen jerseys the boys wore, with the M script on the left breast, embroidered by some of the mothers and aunts and neighbors in the trailing cars, itched at their bony backs, chafed their underarms and necks. The boys wore clean white socks under their baseball leggings. The uniforms were heavily starched, and not yet broken in. Though Mr. Jesse contributed a hefty chunk out of his own pocket, much of the money for their purchase had come from club dues, concession profits from Mohawk Park, where they sold soda and hot dogs during their Sunday afternoon games, and from peanuts roasted in Mr. Jesse's kitchen and peddled at high school football games the previous fall. Their baseball shoes, though not new, were polished and buffed. When they stopped for a pee break at a roadside service station, and the team walked as a unit around back to the colored restroom, the racket they raised sounded like a herd of something hoofed and powerful, the metal spikes clacking against concrete and wood. Ellis, the first team leader, walked at the head of the group, the others in close ranks behind. Bennie and John Lee Cowan, the double-play combination, walked side by side, shortstop John Lee always within a relay's distance to the right of his second baseman. Mr. Jesse taught them to walk with purpose like that, to walk tall, and proud, and together. They were a team now, and a family.

Back out on the road, Highway 98, they drove over Big Creek Lake. The boys looked out over the water. Mr. Jesse and his partner Robert Emanuel talked of fishing. They slowed through the town of Wilmer, wary of police, but not cowed. They were free to ride the same roads as anyone else, as equal there as they found themselves on most baseball diamonds, despite the score—though that freedom was still challenged in 1957, sometimes violently, in Alabama, Mississippi, Arkansas, and Georgia. At the very least, it was still parceled out in too many venues, like restaurants and hotels, bathrooms and water fountains. Mr. Jesse knew to keep a watchful eye out for righteous law enforcement and for angry white folks willing to detour the caravan. Their agenda was baseball. "We're here to play baseball," he told every crowd before every game back on their home field. In his business suit, for he never wore a uniform himself, he made his pronouncement to the fans as they settled in, his players warmed up. "I don't want to see any fighting or drinking, don't want to hear any cussing," he told them, in a gravelly voice that commanded attention. "This is all about your boys," he said. "We're here to play baseball." And then he'd pass around the hat, collecting what funds he could, what substituted for admission and helped subsidize the team.

The move to Mohawk Park, on Ruth Street, in what is now Trinity Gardens, occurred a year earlier. As had happened at the vacant lot on Bullshead, the crowds assembling for their games at Dozier's outgrew the space by the end of their first year there. Over the season of 1955, when they played their first game on Easter Sunday, played until some time after Labor Day, Jesse searched for a suitable replacement. The tract of land at Ruth and First was carved out of a cornfield. The owner agreed to allow the team to set up operations there, allowed them to erect any necessary structures, provided they could be torn down in five to ten days, thinking it was only a temporary venture.

Many teams playing at the time were temporary arrangements. Guys gathered at makeshift ball fields early enough on summer Sunday afternoons, in workpants or dungaree overalls, just looking for an available game. If enough players showed up, they cobbled together two teams, played some unofficiated innings until interest waned or the ball was lost or the light faded from the sky. A whole different collection of players might show up the next week.

The Mohawks were different. They practiced every evening after school and attended the weekly Saturday night meetings at the clubhouse behind Norwood's house. If any player missed either, he was fined and would likely end up benched for the Sunday afternoon game. All the boys wore clean uniforms and Mr. Jesse saw to it that they all had baseball spikes to wear, of one sort or another. They were baseball players, they were Mohawks, he ingrained in them. Part of their job, as baseball players, was to look and act the part.

Their new home, Mohawk Park, reflected that attitude. In an area of the county that had no other civically sponsored recreation facilities, Jesse convinced the city to donate fill dirt to sculpt the diamond. A lumberyard gave the timber and fencing to erect a sturdy, authentic backstop. Jesse bought the wood to build the dugouts, the concession stand, and the bleachers. The boys ran errands and took occasional jobs on Saturday mornings, walking groceries back from the A&P, mowing lawns, or raking leaves, so that they'd have new baseballs to play with come Sunday afternoon. Jesse insisted on all these measures because that's how real baseball organizations conducted themselves. If he couldn't find a real team to play his Mohawks—a team with a roster, coaches, a scorekeeper—they'd practice instead. He'd taken that first full season on Ruth Street arranging road trips, such as the first one to Hattiesburg, making sure the opposing teams met all of his specifications.

When they pulled up to the Hattiesburg field, and the boys filed from the two automobiles, the hometown fans laughed. As Jesse assembled them in front of the third base visitor's dugout, the spectators called out, "What you doing with those little bitty babies?" The Hattiesburg team, the Cardinals, watched, even allowed themselves a laugh or two, at the wide-eyed little boys who'd come to play them. The Cardinals were full-grown men, with facial hair, adult muscles, and plenty of confidence. They swatted batting practice pitches a mile into the Mississippi landscape, threw hard, roping relays back from the outfield, their leather gloves popping when they caught the ball, snickering at the very thought that those boys on the other side would dare challenge them.

Jesse huddled his players around him, said, "Don't you listen to that noise. You're here to play baseball," he reminded them.

"You babies ready?" the opposing pitcher, tall and menacing, called over.

Robert Emanuel led off the game. Swinging at the first pitch, out of excitement, he bounced a dribbler down the third base line. But the Cardinals were playing lazy, cocky defense, with their infielders positioned back safely, outfielders midway, standard. By the time the third baseman picked up the slow roller and rifled it to first, Emanuel, sprinting from the box, was three steps beyond the base. Safe.

It is a cruelty of sports in general, even baseball to some extent, that only the winners, the champions are remembered. Robert Emanuel is a perfect example. In a few years, running for a small black college in Alabama, he would challenge some of the national sprint records that "Bullet" Bob Hayes was establishing while at Florida A&M. Hayes was an Olympic champion, "the fastest man on Earth." Emanuel was that fast, a fact that would cost the Cardinals, but a fact hardly anyone else knew, just as too few people recall that Jackie Robinson's older brother, Mack, took the 200 meter silver medal in the 1936 Berlin

Olympic Games behind Nazi-humbling Jesse Owens.

Emanuel stole second base on the next pitch, a high fastball that Ellis May waved at. Ellis struck out on three more pitches, swinging and missing at a couple of vicious curveballs sandwiched around a heater in the dirt.

With Emanuel dancing off second base, Bennett punched a single through the hole in the right side of the infield where the second baseman was cheating toward the bag behind Emanuel. Jasper followed with a fly ball to center deep enough to allow Emanuel to tag up at third and then score. One-nothing Mohawks.

That was the brand of baseball the Mohawks played, the same methodical yet daring kind of baseball Jackie Robinson introduced to the major leagues, what Durocher alluded to ten years earlier when he berated his petitioning players, "You can't throw him out on the bases; you can't get him out at the plate."

The Mohawks, those little bitty babies, scored three such runs in the first five innings, scratching out single runs in the first, second and fifth frames, running hard, sacrificing, creating and then seizing opportunities. Mr. Jesse taught them textbook, opportunistic baseball, impressing upon them every chance he could, on the practice field, during their meetings, that the secret to baseball, to life in general, was the creation of opportunity. He made sure that the lesson was not lost on those twenty-five young black boys who had absolutely nothing going for them before he came into their lives, reaffirming it each and every time one of them laid down a successful bunt, risked one more step in his lead off the bag, or hit third base with the right foot at the correct speed and location to gain that extra fraction of a second that would let him slide safely home. "The *creation* of opportunity," Jesse would preach, pacing behind the dugout bench, exclamating the point with an index finger. The very condition of freedom, those boys would learn, maybe the most important lesson they could glean from the baseball field, was the creation of opportunity.

The Cardinals failed to score in the bottom halves of those innings, though they hit Jasper very hard. They had men on base every inning but could come no closer to scoring than stranding a runner at third. They never lost their confidence, never stopped acting out for their fans. In the top of the sixth, Bennie Harris was at the plate with two outs. He lofted a two-and-one pitch to left field. It was a routine fly ball, but Bennie set off sprinting down the line toward first. Some of the Cardinals, the pitcher and catcher, the right fielder, started strolling back to their dugout before the ball had even reached its zenith. Harris hit first going full speed and turned toward second. Creating opportunities at every turn meant running hard every time. Bennie was halfway from first to second when the ball dropped into the left fielder's waiting glove and the Cardinals second baseman picked

Bennie up in one beefy arm, lifting Harris off the ground with his legs still churning. The out was made and the Hattiesburg player carried Harris across the infield to the delight of the hometown fans.

Jesse stepped out of the dugout and glanced toward the plate to see if there would be any response to the clowning. The umpire, his mask off, was laughing right along with the rest of them and merely reminded Jesse that he wasn't allowed on the field in street clothes. When Jesse glared back at him, he simply said, "Put down that little bitty baby, Jake."

"Yes sir," Jake said, dropping Harris, to renewed hoots and screams of laughter.

Jesse knew at that moment he would not bring his Mohawks back to play this team, but he would offer no more protest than that. "Way to hustle," he said to Harris, patting him on the shoulder.

The Mohawks laugh about the episode themselves, now. Ellis May, the Candyman, saying, "You shoulda seen Bennie's legs just a-digging," imitating the motion, wiggling the two first fingers of his right hand.

"They drop that ball, I'm on second base," Bennie says, defending himself.

"Until they snatched you, right up off the ground."

"I *was* kind of little," Harris offers.

"Shoot," Madison chimes in, "You *still* little."

The rest of the Mohawks chuckle at that, including Harris, and even Lomax, though he hides his mouth behind a closed hand, as if he's coughing quietly and not laughing.

Then Pugh straightens himself in his chair, ready to offer one of his rare contributions. "But you was a magician on the pivot," he tells Bennie.

"Yeah," Emanuel, Madison, and others murmur in agreement, "That's right."

"A *wizard*," May says, facing forward, not teasing his old friend and teammate anymore, but making a kind of gospel pronouncement. "A wizard."

Bennie dips his head and nods to the sentiment and glances to his right, where John Lee would be, as if to emphasize the point that he certainly didn't do it by himself.

Harris and Cowan had first studied the double play, "the pitcher's best friend," from a book Jesse provided them, a book coauthored by Pee Wee Reese, Jackie Robinson's double-play partner, a combo Kahn considers the greatest of the era. "Study this," said Mr. Jesse, turning to that chapter of baseball fundamentals. And they did, together, taking turns reading the text, the captions, while the other looked at the pictures. Then they practiced the maneuvers endlessly, long after regular practice was over for the day. They flipped the ball to each other from all distances spread out around the middle of the infield—sidearm, overhand, underhand. They practiced dragging their toes across the bag and throwing over to first in one fluid motion, aiming for a metal trash can substituting as a first baseman since all the other Mohawks had wandered off home, the sound of a baseball rattling around in there echoing into the evening. They practiced leading each other with their tosses, catching them barehanded, practiced crossing paths on ground balls up the middle of the field. They got so they knew exactly where the other would be on any given play, exactly what kind of throw to expect, a choreography of shared consciousness, a kind of magician's act.

Even now, when Harris glances to the empty chair beside him, it's as though he's responding to some movement of Cowan's, six hundred miles away, reaching for a glass of tea, maybe, or picking up one of those menthol cigarettes he took to smoking in later years.

The Cardinals broke through in their half of the sixth, their second baseman clubbing a home run so far over Emanuel's head that he was already strutting and bowing his way down the third base line by the time Emanuel could chase it down, as fast as he was. It took another few minutes for the crowd, the rest of the Cardinals, to settle back down, calling to each other, "Did you *see* that?" swooning and hollering out, "Mercy!"

Mr. Jesse changed pitchers. He could see Jasper was tiring and brought in Lomax, just fourteen, the youngest player on the team. Lomax could throw hard, but had little else in his arsenal yet. The Mohawk defense backed up, Cowan and Harris playing deep in the holes of the infield, Pugh backing up along the third base line, trying to protect their three-to-one lead. Coach Lomax, Willie's uncle, positioned the outfielders deeper still, and Norwood replaced his right and left fielders, May and Bennett, with the fastest players he had left, Rembert and Brown, sacrificing any potential offensive output in an effort to hold the Hattiesburg team. The Cardinals, bigger, stronger, natural fastball hitters, clobbered young Lomax's pitches, as if it was batting practice all over again, lofting fly balls the Mohawk outfielders had to scurry to get under. The Hattiesburg fans called out, "Good-bye," each time one of those monstrous shots left the bat, only to register their surprise when Emanuel or Rembert somehow managed to catch the thing, grumbling, "Oh, man."

Had there been a fence around the field, the final score might have been twenty to three. As it was, the speedy Mohawks outfielders limited the Cardinals to another solo shot in the seventh, and a two-run homer in the bottom of the eighth.

In the top of the ninth, their team down by a run, the very bottom of the Mohawk order was due up, Bennie Harris. He popped a foul ball up to the catcher. That brought up Emanuel, who once again turned a ground ball into an infield single, though his legs were aching from roaming all over the outfield tracking down those batted meteors. Rembert followed. He brought less of a bat to the plate than May, but it was exactly the situation Jesse had anticipated. He signaled Rembert to bunt, playing for just the one run, to tie the game, hoping for another chance to win if they could just hang around long enough. Rembert bunted the pitch softly down the first base line. The Cardinal defense rotated slowly, a little confused, and had no play on Emanuel at second. It was a near perfect sacrifice bunt. And while Jesse Norwood, not normally given to demonstrative exhibitions one way or the other, clapped his appreciation for Rembert's execution of the play, Coach Emanuel came charging down the third base line to meet Rembert as he returned to the bench and bear-hugged his player as if he'd walloped one of those tape measure home runs instead of laying down the sacrifice. The play, and the Mohawk coach's reaction, quieted the home crowd some. They may just then have begun to realize they were witnessing genuine, precision baseball.

Willie Lomax, in Jasper's spot in the order, batted next. Again, even though Lomax was younger, not yet developed, Jesse knew he was a gamer, and couldn't have asked for a better matchup, as if he had somehow predicted this situation two and a half innings earlier when he'd made the changes. Lomax would take a lot of pitches. He had that good an eye at the plate, one of the reasons Jesse was certain he would develop into such a good pitcher. The Hattiesburg pitcher, though bigger and stronger, had been in there the entire game, and must have been getting a little tired. This was one of the marks of the Mohawks' baseball. The players might have been little bitty babies compared to the men they played against, but Jesse had enough of them, knew their relative skills, and kept them fresh, kept them situationally prepared. Other teams rarely brought more than the minimum number of necessary players, ten, eleven at most, to cover sudden injuries only. They saw themselves as a group of players, and if baseball was the game, they wanted to be on the field, in on the action at every possible moment. Jesse Norwood platooned his players and always had something in reserve. While his boys were as eager to play as anybody else on any other team, they'd been groomed in a team approach to the game all along. They'd grown to understand, even as early as thirteen, fourteen, fifteen years old, through the team meetings, the "fifteen minutes of baseball and forty-five minutes of life," that there was a larger purpose here than just their individual athletic development. Jesse stressed that fundamental skills were but parts of a bigger package, components of a complete baseball player, a rounded human being, a contributor to society. Jesse told them, in fact, during practices, once he had assessed their particular skills, how he would someday use one or the other of them, as the best, most logical candidate to get the job done. He said to Rembert, for instance, "I want you to work on that bunting. We're going to need that in a game." He might have said to Lomax, as he was selecting a bat there in Hattiesburg, "Make him throw you your pitch."

Lomax took the first pitch, a fastball, for a strike. Then he fouled off two more heaters to the right, just not strong enough to muscle the ball into play, but not missing by much. With two strikes on him, the Hattiesburg team, their fans, sensed victory, even started celebrating, calling out, "Time to go home, babies."

The pitcher, already counting his win, tried to waste a curveball, missing wide, the ball skipping under the catcher's glove. Emanuel scampered to third on the wild pitch. Lomax fouled off three more pitches, the third one a line drive over first base that sliced just foul. The eighth offering was another curve that missed inside, Lomax dancing out of the way. He stepped back into the box, taking up a stance as forward as possible, crowding the plate, to give himself every inch of advantage.

Concern registered on the pitcher's face, replacing the smirk that had been there. He couldn't get his fastball by Lomax, he couldn't get his curve over the plate, and there was no relief in sight. If he lost his lead now, all those fans who had been hooting and hollering throughout the afternoon would turn their derision on him. Together, Emanuel and Lomax were a composite Jackie Robinson, according to Durocher's definition that night in the kitchen during spring training in 1947, which was precisely the Mohawk way.

The Cardinal's pitcher reared back once more but overthrew the ball, squeezing too hard, trying to overpower Lomax, and it bounced in the dirt in front of the plate, dribbling beneath the catcher. Emanuel almost broke for home, but thought better of it as the catcher dove for the ball and the pitcher ran in to cover. The catcher walked to the mound, said, "Settle down, Petey, and get this kid out," while his pitcher paced behind the mound, rubbing up the baseball, trying to compose himself. Full count, 3 and 2.

Jesse Norwood's little bitty Mohawks had the team from Hattiesburg unnerved. It was victory enough in his eyes, that his players, as young as they were, as small as they were, could work themselves to this critical moment.

Willie Lomax readied himself at the plate for the tenth pitch in the sequence. Nearly everyone at the game expected another fastball. This war had become such a point of honor for the Hattieburg team they couldn't even afford to lose this minor skirmish, couldn't afford to walk Lomax, especially with Pugh on deck, who'd already knocked in a run that afternoon. The pitcher stood on the mound, ball behind his back, looking in for a sign: fastball. He gripped the ball, wrapping his index and middle fingers across two of the red seams, the other two fingers and thumb spread to either side. He wound up, kicked, and fired home. The ball started trailing down and away from Lomax early, starting nearly as high as his shoulders before sliding down into the strike zone. Anticipating the pitch, Lomax had to commit and swing early, to have any chance of delivering any power through the bat to the ball. He got out in front of it and connected at the weakest point of his swing, just hard enough to loop a soft fly ball over the left side of the infield. The Cardinal defense had long since shifted the other way, after Lomax had fouled so many pitches to the right. Emanuel, unchecked at third because of the shift, taking a liberal lead down the line, ran on contact. The ball floated over the outstretched glove of the leaping third baseman. The shortstop, leaning right, stumbled trying to reverse direction, and the left fielder broke straight in from his position after taking one reflexive step backward in response to the force of Lomax's swing. Emanuel crossed the plate in time to stop and turn and watch the left fielder and the short-stop both race to get under the ball. He even allowed himself a little triumphant leap when he saw the shortstop hurl himself. Emanuel landed back on the loose dirt behind home plate in the same instant the ball dropped into the shortstop's outstretched glove. Lomax was out. Game over. Willie stopped running, after making the turn around first base. He hung his head and trotted back across the infield toward the visitor's dugout.

"But," one of the Mohawk faithful sitting in a lawn chair behind their bench protested as the teams left the field, "Robert scored!"

"Don't count," a more knowledgeable fan answered.

The celebration on the other side of the field, while still loud, even boisterous, was tinged with relief. The fans clapped and hugged each other, a few older men returned to the barbecue spits back by picnic tables loaded down with salads and casseroles and cakes, to tend to the chicken and ribs that had been left alone to cook throughout the last inning. Cardinal players acknowledged each other's efforts and headed in the direction of a cold drink and some food, but not before passing close enough by the subdued Mohawks to tell them, "Nice game, guys."

Jesse, having bagged up their equipment, moved in front of his team, walked the length of the bench, calling each of their names so they'd look up and into his eyes. "Be proud of yourselves, gentlemen. You played a *great* game out there," he said. "We'll talk about it next week. For now, let's get something to eat."

Ellis May, sitting at the table with his eyes closed, his face lifted, inhales deeply, as if he can summon to mind the pungent sauce mixed in with the smoke wafting off the cooking meat that day back in 1957. He exhales. "We won respect," he says, no matter the final score. Some of their fans briefly debated the point of Emanuel's scoring, but the boys, already students of the game, knew better, though in deference to the adults, wouldn't argue with them, wouldn't so much as answer back, something else they picked up from Mr. Jesse. It's part of the game.

"Losing after great striving," Roger Kahn called it, "the story of man, who was born to sorrow, whose sweetest songs tell of saddest thought, and who, if he is a hero, does nothing in life as becomingly as leaving it."[22]

The men gathered in the Trinity Gardens Recreation Center nod in agreement with May's declaration about winning respect. These former Mohawks, many of whom were there that day, know full well that in baseball—where the defense has control of the ball, where hitting that ball is acknowledged to be the most difficult thing in sport, where even if you do, it doesn't count an overwhelming majority of the time, doesn't count until the ball is rendered fair—whatever happens until the ball is called fair, likewise, doesn't count. And that, they have learned, through their baseball careers, over the course of their lives, seems as much as anyone can reasonably expect—a chance to put the ball in play, a fair chance. And they'll say that they also learned through those many, many years of meetings, where a little bit of baseball applied to a lot of life, that maybe there is a life's lesson in the game, that maybe, like baseball, it's not about running out of time, or fair chances. Those are factors that can't be controlled. You only exhaust outs, innings, and times at bat, opportunities to make something happen, whether it's a sacrifice or a home run. The best thing any of them could do would be to keep up with the game well enough to make sure they're ready for their next turn, each turn.

Four

*I*n a game so thoroughly imbued with statistics, from its understanding to its appreciation to its moment-by-moment strategy, managers and coaches and players are constantly playing percentages, as much as they are playing against each other. Nearly every single facet of every single play in the game is one of applying those percentages in order to accentuate or retard the possibility of success. You can't bulldog your way down the field or sprint up the diamond in order to score in baseball. Sheer physical force of strength or speed or even willpower rarely constitutes an advantage that can't be overcome and defeated by subtle manipulation of those percentages. An overpowering pitcher can be worn down and outlasted. Any single dominant batter can be neutralized in critical situations, through the artful application of percentages. That application is the primary responsibility of the field manager, who brings to the dugout a thorough enough understanding of the parameters of the game and the data points of each of the players on the field and in reserve, a compilation of statistics called "baseball wisdom."

It's a peculiarity of baseball, and one of the reasons it has seeped so far beyond the ball field into the fabric of Americana, this reliance on statistics and percentages. Unlike other major American sports, there have been no revolutionizing innovations in baseball, such as the single-wing running formation of football or the triangle offense in basketball. The rules and rudimentary skills of baseball have remained relatively unchanged through the decades. The fundamentals of the game are learned at the earliest introduction to the sport. That's what makes it possible for a team of little bitty babies from Prichard, Alabama, to compete with grown men in Hattiesburg. The outcome of any particular baseball game often turns on the smallest of factors.

Conventional baseball wisdom says the visiting team should always play for the go-ahead run, because the visiting team runs out of innings, which is to say, opportunities, first. It seems an obvious, simple matter, but it wasn't always the case. In the earliest days of the game, the home team chose whether it wanted to bat first or last. The number of balls or strikes determining a walk or an out shifted periodically. Pitchers threw underhanded, and the batter was allowed to call for a preferred location of the pitch, either high or low, and if he fouled that pitch off, it didn't always count as a strike against him.

Various writers and historians locate 1903 as the beginning of the "modern era" of baseball. That was the year of the signing of the "National Agreement," recognizing the upstart American League of teams as a co-equal to the elder National League after it adopted the same foul-strike rules. It was the first year a "world series" was played to determine the game's overall champion between the best teams from each league (the American's Boston franchise squared off against the National's Pittsburgh). This modern era came nearly sixty years after the game's "invention," when one of the most pivotal (and mystical) parameters of the game—the distance between bases, ninety feet—was established by Alexander Cartwright. Overhand pitching was only "allowed" almost forty years later, in 1884. This led, necessarily, to the definition of a strike zone and canceled the batter's freedom to call for a preferred location of a pitch. Thus baseball distinguished itself from any other game, insofar as the defense controls the ball. This relationship between offense and defense may be as responsible as anything else about the game for its metaphoric utility in so many other facets of life. Rules further defining that relationship quickly followed: three strikes as an out in 1888, and four balls a walk the following year. The most important parameter of this relationship between pitcher and batter materialized four years later in 1893, when the distance separating the two was lengthened from fifty feet to the inspired number of sixty feet, six inches. After that there were but a few more adjustments governing the batter's chances—

when a fouled ball counts as a strike (the first two) or not, and the special circumstance of a fouled bunt attempt for a third strike—until the competitive agreement in 1903, by which time the home team always batted last.[23]

To the casual observer, most of the game of baseball seems like a simple matter, a basic, fundamental progression of throwing the ball, hitting the ball, and catching the ball. But by sacrificing the second out in the top of the ninth to move Emanuel from first to second base, Jesse Norwood was essentially playing to tie the game. Hattiesburg, the home team, could then come to bat in their half of the inning with a chance to win the game on one swing of the bat. That reconfigures the percentages and puts all the pressure on the Mohawk pitcher, on young Lomax, who can't, in a tie game in the bottom of the ninth, afford any mistakes. As difficult as it is to hit a baseball, batters seize any advantage available, any advantage, even one as subtle as knowing the pitcher will be pitching cautiously. If he's too cautious, of course, he'll walk a batter, or two, putting the winning run on base—a thing *conventional* baseball wisdom dictates should never be done—changing the whole dynamic of the game with each pitch. All the pressure's on the next pitch. Unbeknownst to those same casual observers, the ball feels a little heavier, the strike zone shrinks, and the bat looks bigger and quicker.

"Looks like a big ol' tennis racket up there," Lomax grumbles.

Some of the others chuckle.

"What you got to remember," Candyman says, holding up his hand, "is that was our first road trip. We was *young*."

"Little bitty babies," Pugh says, in a deep unbabyish voice.

"There would come a time," Candyman goes on, leaning back in his chair, folding his arms across his chest, "a *time*, when big league prospects would be *begging* Shoe to throw them something they could hit."

Lomax looks down at his feet. Rather than speak to that claim, he says instead, "I didn't get a hit that day, so it really don't matter now."

Other players in the room, Emanuel, May, Sellers, even Campbell, who really was a little bitty baby at the time, look as if they're still waiting for that one more chance, would still put their odds of succeeding up against anyone else's.

Because there would come a time too, not long after that initial trip to Hattiesburg, when the Mohawks would string together near-perfect seasons. Each of them, independently, talk of seasons as early as 1959 and 1960, seasons with 30 wins and 4 losses, 35 and 3, regularly compiling .900 winning percentage years. And they took on all comers, Jesse Norwood requiring only that the teams have coaches and score-keepers—organizational prerequisites, insisting on a professional and serious approach to the game—not giving a second thought to how talented an opponent might be. They played against teams boasting former big leaguers, against white all-star teams from north Alabama. They played the nearby Atmore prison team yearly, a team of much older and stronger men, not unlike that Hattiesburg team. The only such team to play games on the prison grounds, Jesse's boys were taken there for both the competitive and cautionary experience.

"There's a lot of us that could have ended up inside," Willie Lomax says, and you can't quite believe he's including himself as an example, but he is.

"Easily," Madison agrees.

"But not one of us did," May says. "Not *one*!"

The not-so-subtle practice of taking those boys to the prison games ended only after there was an attempted escape during one of the contests. Mr. Jesse said he didn't want any part of that, and he quit scheduling the exhibitions.

They played and eventually beat the semipro Prichard Athletics, one of the oldest and most successful and vaunted teams in the area, claiming for the Mohawks a supremacy the Athletics had held for decades. They played university teams and teams boasting future big-league stars like Tommie Aaron, Cleon Jones, Tommie Agee, and Amos Otis, and won.

"Them Mobile Bears," May says, speaking of the Dodgers' AA affiliate Mobile Bears, "they *refused* to play us!"

But it's that Hattiesburg game they talk about, when they're all together, for whatever reason, baseball men that they are, speaking to how close-knit a team they became, even as early as 1957. Losing games, they knew by then, came down to a few minor events turning the tables. They learned more from studying those smaller aspects, the misplaced pitch, the line drives barely dropping foul, the missed cutoff man, the failed sacrifice, became better baseball players by studying those.

The 1951 National League pennant race, one that "belongs to the ages," Roger Kahn reports, came down to a series of such pressure pitches and minor events. The Brooklyn Dodgers and the New York Giants had finished the regular season with identical records. The pennant was to be decided by a best two-out-of-three playoff. The Giants won the first game, followed by a Dodgers shutout. The next day, October 3, at the Polo Grounds, Giants home field, with one out in the bottom of the ninth of the third and deciding game, leading 4 to 2, two runners on base, Ralph Branca, of the Dodgers, was brought in to pitch to Bobby Thomson. Don Newcombe and the Dodgers started the inning leading 4 to 1, having broken a 1-to-1 tie the inning before. Newcombe had pitched the whole game, and was still throwing strong. With two quick strikes on him, Alvin Dark, the leadoff hitter for the Giants, "rapped a bounder into the hole in the right side of the infield. Both Hodges and Robinson broke for the ball and Newcombe ran to cover first base. Hodges, straining, touched the ball with the tip of his mitt and deflected it away from Robinson. Perhaps if Hodges had not touched it, Robinson could have made the play. As it was, Dark reached first. A single, ruled the scorer."[24]

Then, Kahn reports, Dodger manager Dressen "made a curious decision. He let Hodges hold the bag on Dark, as though Dark as a base runner were important. Actually, of course, Dark could have stolen second, third, and home without affecting the game. The Giants needed three runs to tie, not one, and the Dodgers needed outs."[25]

Sure enough, the next batter, Don Mueller, bounced a single through the right side, through the space vacated by Hodges, where, if he'd been normally positioned, he might have made the play, might have even turned a double play. Baseball revisionism is an off-season staple of the "hot-stove" leagues. And while it probably is true, as Leonard Koppett puts it, that "every player, in his secret heart, wants to manage someday" and "every fan, in the privacy of his mind, already does,"[26] no one can really say what decision they would have made in that situation, or whether a different strategy would have made any difference. Mueller, for instance, said, "I don't agree that if Hodges had played me deep rather than holding

Dark at the bag, the outcome would have been different." Well known for his skilled place hitting, Mueller makes a claim that has more than a little substance: "If Hodges had played deep, I would have swung differently and just as likely gotten a base hit."[27]

Runners were at first and third, Monte Irvin coming to bat. Branca was reportedly "fast and loose" in the bullpen. Dressen called time and walked to the mound to confer. The change he was considering making was behind the plate, bringing in Roy Campanella to replace Rube Walker, because, Kahn writes, "Campanella had a way with Newcombe." But Campy had a bum leg, so Dressen chose not to replace the more agile Walker. "When Irvin fouled out to Hodges, Dressen decided that he had done the right thing,"[28] in his subtle playing of the percentages.

Then Whitey Lockman doubled to left, scoring Dark. The tally was now 4 to 2. Two runners on, only one out, with Bobby Thomson coming to bat. Branca was ready. Dressen brought him in.

"Get him out" was Dressen's only instruction for his pitcher, handing him the ball.

Branca's first pitch to Thomson was a fastball over the inside part of the plate. Thomson watched it for a strike, exactly how Branca wanted to start him. Then he wanted to throw Thomson another fastball, higher, and tighter, even wasting a pitch in order to set up a curveball low and away. But Thomson swung at the pitch, swung hard, driving it to left. The ball sailed over shortstop Pee Wee Reese's head *and* the left fielder's head and disappeared over the eighteen-foot-high left field fence, deep into the seats, above the 315-foot sign. Home run. The "shot heard 'round the world!" Giants win the ballgame, 5 to 4. More important, "The Giants win the pennant! The Giants win the pennant! The Giants win the pennant!"

The game had been televised coast to coast, and the moment of Thomson's home run has been burned into the national consciousness ever since, with its telling and retelling. It is a moment with very few equals in American sports. There are not many people, baseball fan or no, who can't identify the radio broadcaster Russ Hodges's dramatic call, "The Giants win the pennant!" And yet that moment was set up by the deflection of a routine infield ground ball, a defiance of the percentages of player positioning, and a second-guessed pitch selection.

Kahn reports that "Jackie Robinson said he did not remember Branca's first pitch to Thomson as being hip-high on the inside. 'I thought it was right down the middle. I remember, Pee Wee and I exchanged looks. Like, if Branca throws another like that, we're cooked.'"[29]

About that next pitch, teammate Sal Maglie challenged Branca years later:

"'How were you pitching to Thomson?'"

'I wanted to get ahead of him,' Branca said, 'throw a strike.'

'You did get ahead of him,' Maglie said. 'Then what?'

'I wanted to get him with a curve. I threw the second fastball to set up a curve.'

'If you wanted to get him with a curve in a spot like that,' Maglie said, 'you should have thrown the curve. What were you waiting for?'

Branca did not argue."[30]

Baseball. And percentages.

What's not as well remembered is the fact that there probably should never have been a playoff series at all. On August 11, the Dodgers split a doubleheader against the Braves. At the end of the day they were thirteen games ahead of the Giants in the standings. Over the last six weeks of the season Brooklyn played five-hundred ball, losing a game for every win. The Giants won five for every game they lost, making up an average of two games a week, and on September 30, the last day of the season, when they beat the Braves, they finished with a half-game lead for the pennant. Brooklyn was still playing its final game in Philadelphia. In that game, the Dodgers made a miraculous comeback, and the score was tied after nine innings. Extra innings. In the bottom of the twelfth, Jackie made a game-saving catch on an injury-defying stab of a ball lined back up the middle that left him prostrate in the dirt, the wind knocked out of him, his ribs bruised. The Dodgers finally won 9 to 8, after Jackie Robinson's home run in the top of the fourteenth inning.

"Just goes to show ya," Brooklyn's publicity man Irving Rudd said. "If a ballgame lasts long enough, Jackie Robinson will win it for ya."[31]

It simply was not in Jackie Robinson's constitution to quit, or to yield to defeat without a challenge. At the end of that historic ball game on October 3, 1951, with Bobby Thomson dancing around the bases, skipping and leaping, most of the Dodgers were headed off the field, walking toward the distant centerfield clubhouse before Thomson reached second base, their season over. Not Jackie Robinson. He stayed in the infield and followed Thomson's circuit. "He wanted to make sure Thomson touched all bases before conceding that the pennant race was over."[32]

Jackie's vigilance had historical precedent, which he might have known about. The Giants had been involved in another famous pennant-deciding game back in 1908, "the most storied game in baseball history until Bobby Thomson's homer," Koppett writes. "On September 23 the Cubs and the Giants were playing their final scheduled game against each other, at the Polo Grounds…. Fred Merkle, a rookie first baseman, singled with two out in the ninth inning of a 1-1 game, sending a teammate from first to third. When Al Bridwell lined a single to center, the winning run came in from third, the crowd started to pour out of the stands. Merkle, who had vacated first base on Birdwell's hit, did what almost all players did in those days—he didn't bother to touch second base but sprinted for the clubhouse in center field to avoid being engulfed by the crowd."[33]

This became forever known as "Merkle's boner."

According to the rules of the game, if the Cubs got the ball to second, Merkle would be forced out, for the third out, and the run wouldn't count. In the chaos, no one really knows for sure what happened, but the Cubs claimed they did get the ball to second, and the umpires later decided the run was nullified, declaring the game still tied. It would have to be replayed entirely if it was necessary to decide the outcome of the pennant race, which it was, on October 8. The Cubs won 4 to 2, robbing the Giants of the pennant.

In 1951, Jackie Robinson stayed on the field and watched Bobby Thomson touch all four bases. He had fulfilled his three-year promise to Branch Rickey to turn the other cheek and not respond to the prejudicial taunting he was constantly subjected to. He would take it upon himself to ensure that every last letter of the rulebook had been satisfied before he would concede, and he would raise his singular voice in protest if he needed to, for he knew the rules that well. He had to. For the first three years of his major league career, the narrow confines of the game's rules were the only areas he was allowed to operate in. Outside of those rules, Jackie was muted, by design, by Rickey.

The story goes that Branch Rickey's motivation to integrate baseball can be traced back to 1903, the year the game achieved two-league stability. He was the coach of the Ohio Wesleyan University baseball team. That team included one black player, Charles "Cha" Thomas. When they traveled to South Bend, Indiana, to play Notre Dame, a desk clerk at the team hotel told Thomas he couldn't stay there. "We provide accommodations only for white people." With some effort, Rickey cajoled the clerk into allowing Thomas to bunk in his room.

"Upstairs, Thomas began to weep. As Rickey recounted the scene, 'His shoulders heaved, and he rubbed one great hand over the other with all the power of his body, muttering, "Black skin…black skin. If I could only make it white." He was trying literally to claw the black skin off his bones."

When Rickey told Kahn the story, "tears appeared in *his* eyes. Signing Jackie Robinson, he said, was a way of trying to make things right for his old and wounded Wesleyan friend, Cha Thomas."[34]

Forty years and two World Wars later, little, if anything had changed, despite the enthusiastic patriotism and valor displayed by hundreds of thousands of black men and women during those wars. In World War I alone, heeding W. E. B. DuBois's call to "forget our special grievances and close ranks...with our white fellow citizens,"[35] over a quarter-million black soldiers answered the call to arms. Those black soldiers did not reap any domestic benefit for their effort though. "Black patriotism had little effect on convincing the federal government to dismantle Jim Crow and stem the rising tide of white supremacy."[36]

What's more, the summer after that war, the time of year for baseball, the national pastime, what's been called the "Red Summer" of 1919, Du Bois would come to regret his clarion call to "close ranks," after seventy blacks were lynched, including ten uniformed soldiers. Jackie Robinson's father disappeared that year, ran out on his wife and five children. Jackie Robinson and Jesse Norwood were both still babies. The "Black Sox" scandal rocked the baseball world that fall, though baseball would recover soon enough. The Yankees acquired Babe Ruth the next year. His home run production brought fans back to the game in droves. The plight of black players would not change so easily, not until another war was waged, not until Wesley Branch Rickey, among others, fought for the signing of Robinson and the integration of major league baseball.

But Jackie nearly quit during the first month of his major league career. Philadelphia came to Ebbets Field for a three-game series against the Dodgers in late April 1947. Tennessee-born and Alabama-raised Ben Chapman was the manager of the Phillies. Chapman was unconditionally bigoted. He disliked Jews and *hated* "nigras."

"Hey, black boy. Snowflake," he started calling out to Robinson from the moment they took the field. "When did they let you outa the jungle?"

"All my life I've been a proud guy," Kahn reports Jackie as saying. "I won't sit in the back of the bus," an attribute that nearly cost him his commission during the war. "If you call me nigger or boy, I want to tear your throat out. I'm a proud guy.

"So there I am in Brooklyn, which is supposed to be the Promised Land, and I'm hearing the worst garbage I ever heard in my whole life, counting the streets, counting the army, but I've sworn to Mr. Rickey that I won't fight back.

"So I play ball, but they don't stop. Jungle bunny. Snowflake. I start breathing hard. I'm just playing ball. I'm doing my job. I'm a good ballplayer. Deep down, I've been thinking, people will see I'm a good ballplayer and they'll see I'm black and they'll put that together. A black guy's a good ballplayer. A black guy can be a good guy."[37]

But that didn't happen. Chapman and some of the other Phillies were unrelenting in their abuse. Typically in baseball, bantering, even vulgar bantering, is common, though it usually goes both ways. That day the rest of the Dodgers, whether Northerners or Southerners, were shocked into the same muted silence, as if they too had been counseled against responding. Jackie nearly cracked:

"All of a sudden I thought, the hell with this. This isn't me. They're making me be some crazy pacifist black freak. Hell, no. Hell, no. I'm going back to being myself. Right now. I'm going into the Phillie dugout and grab one of those white sons of bitches and smash his fucking teeth and walk away. Walk away from this ballpark. Walk away from baseball.

"I thought some more. This didn't take as long in my head as it takes to tell you, Rog. I thought of Mr. Rickey and Rae and my baby son. Standing on that ballfield in Brooklyn, standing still, I had come to a crossroads.

"For a second I felt, this is it. I'm cracking up."[38]

At that point in the young season, even though Jackie had been responsible for the only run in Brooklyn's one-to-nothing victory, his major league career, the success of Rickey's "experiment," the whole question of integration was in peril.

The next day, when Jackie came to bat in the first inning, Chapman resumed the assault. "Hey, jungle bunny."

Other Dodgers complained to the press, which, Kahn writes, "persisted in its belligerent neutrality." Manager Burt Shotton informed his boss. Something had to be done, Rickey is reported as complaining to commissioner Chandler, in the name of decency. Chandler's action isn't worth mentioning, not in any discussion of disciplinary effectiveness. In May, the Dodgers were scheduled to play a series in Philadelphia. The Phillies general manager, Herb Pennock, got in on the bigoted mischief, warning Rickey that he wouldn't field a team against his Brooklyn club if it included "that boy."

Rickey responded that he would gladly accept the victories by forfeiture. The games were played, and Chapman continued, now aiming abuse also at Jackie's teammates, yelling at Pee Wee Reese, Jackie's double-play partner. "Hey, Pee Wee. Yeah, you. Reese. How ya like playin' with a fuckin' nigger?"[39]

Reese responded by trotting over to Jackie and draping his arm around Robinson's shoulders, all the while staring into the dugout at Chapman. But it took bitter complaining from those teammates to move someone with authority to silence Chapman finally. Curiously, Robinson's most vociferous supporter at the time was second baseman Eddie Stanky. "The Phillies are a disgrace," he told the New York press. "They're gutless." This from a Philadelphia native, who had moved to Mobile, where he would forge his own baseball legacy as a college coach after retiring from the game. In the intervening years Stanky harassed Robinson himself after losing his job to him. "But in May 1947 something deep and good was touched within Eddie Stanky, a combative, thin-lipped, verbal ballplayer with limited skills and limitless fire."[40]

The most serious threat to Rickey's experiment came from the organization that he had built into a perennial pennant contender through an innovative farm team system, defending champion St. Louis Cardinals. Rickey was the architect of the famous Gashouse Gang of the 1930s, which included "Dizzy" Dean, Pepper Martin, Joe Medwick, Frankie Frisch, and Durocher. The influence of his system was still evident in the team that had already won four pennants and the World Series in three of those years, from 1942, the year he left, to 1946. Some of the Cardinal players, along with Chapman, Jackie's then teammate "Dixie" Walker, and other "redneck" players throughout the National League, conspired to organize a strike on May 20, 1947, refusing to take an integrated field. They would bring baseball to a halt and try to drive Robinson from the game. Ford Frick, the president of the league, got wind of the scheme, and counseled the individuals involved that if they went ahead with their plan, they would be suspended from the league. His unyielding message was this: "You will find if you go through with your intention that you will have been guilty of complete madness."[41]

The rebellion was averted.

The story of Frick's decisive action reached Stanley

Woodward of the *Herald Tribune*, whose reports generated a backlash of publicity that effectively squashed
what Woodward called "further strolls down Tobacco
Road." That autumn Woodward's exposure of the story
won him a Dutton Award for best sports reporting. By
then, Robinson had won Rookie of the Year honors,
validating his success. He and Rickey had changed the
course of American race relations. "In this strange
moment," David Falkner writes of Jackie's rookie
season, "it seemed that history could be shaped to the
contours of a baseball field."[42]

For his part, Jackie Robinson didn't consider himself finally accepted as a ballplayer until a particular
game a few years later, a game he was thrown out of.
An umpire tossed him from the game for arguing a
call, not because of the color of his skin. The distinction predated King's "I have a dream" speech, delivered the summer of 1963, by more than a decade.
Only then did Robinson consider himself on equal
ground, or on a level playing field, whether at
Brooklyn's Ebbets Field or Shibe Park in Philadelphia,
or even the Polo Grounds across the river in New
York, where he could stand his ground and monitor
Bobby Thomson's gleeful circuit around the bases.
But, it has been noted, Jackie was the only Dodger
player to venture into the Giant clubhouse to congratulate the team on their victory, too, as a baseball
ambassador more than anything else.

The division between white and black, "the veil,"
as DuBois had first characterized it, had seemingly
been lifted. "More formidable, more subtle than a barrier or wall, which could after all be dismantled, the
veil promoted visual distortion even as it created separation. On one side there was light, visibility, and on
the other side darkness and obscurity."[43]

Only once the veil had been lifted could Jackie or
any other black ballplayer be judged by the content of
his baseball character. And there were others: Newcombe, Campanella, and Doby immediately after
Robinson, and many, many others.

The great crusader, Branch Rickey, was gone,
leveraged out of the Dodger organization by Walter
O'Malley after the 1950 season. He was brought to
Pittsburg to re-create the farm systems he'd designed
in St. Louis, and then Brooklyn. His efforts eventually
succeeded with a Pirate World Series victory in 1960.
Rickey had resigned five years earlier, though many of
the scouts and executives he'd brought from Brooklyn
were still there. Finally, twenty years after he'd left the
organization, he returned to St. Louis—which hadn't
won a pennant since "the boys from the Hookworm
Belt" won it all back in 1946—in 1962. In the strange
compression of repetitive history, the Cardinals won
the series in 1964 with Rickey as an advisor, and then
they promptly fired him. He died a little over a year
later, not quite eighty-four-years old.

Jackie, who had survived the tumultuous assaults

of those early years with grace and dignity, stood his ground on the Polo Grounds infield amid the maelstrom of New York's pennant celebration that October day in 1951, a conquering hero to millions of blacks across the country, ready to carry the mantle he'd so courageously won. Twelve hundred miles away, from an infield at old Prichard Stadium in Alabama, scrawny seventeen-year-old Henry Aaron, just one of those many, many others, would follow Jackie's lead into professional baseball the next summer.

Part-time scout for the Indianapolis Clowns and former player for the Norfolk All-Stars of the Negro League, eighty-six-year-old Edward Scott never tires of telling the story. "I told my wife I was going to go to a softball game. She said, 'Why are you going to a softball game? You're not going to find any baseball players out there.'

"I was living in Toulminville and they were playing a fast-pitch softball game. I saw this kid ripping this fast-pitch softball. I asked him after the game, 'Do you play baseball?' He said he did. I said, 'How about coming out to Prichard and playing with the Athletics?' He said, 'Will you get me a suit?' I said, 'Yeah, I'll get you a suit.' So he said he would."[44]

Scott's "attention was captured not only by the hitting ability, but also by the odd way the young swinger gripped the bat with crisscrossed hands,"[45] something Aaron has attributed to his time spent swinging at fluttering bottle caps.

Young Henry played baseball, played softball, played corkball. When he couldn't find a game going on, he played by himself in his backyard, swatting at a wad of bound rags with a stick. He'd been swinging at anything he could find and dreaming of becoming a big-league ballplayer as long as he could remember. Three months after his eighteenth birthday, five years after the foiled insurrections of Dixie Walker and other racist ballplayers had failed to chase Robinson from the game, it looked like Henry might get his chance, though it wouldn't be quite so easy. Henry's folks took some convincing. The greatest home run hitter the sport has seen was almost kept from the game by concerned, fearful parents who hoped to shield him from the abuse he would certainly encounter. They had told him when he was younger that there would *never* be any black major league players. They had grown up listening to stories of slavery and reconstruction, in the midst of Jim Crow and the Klan. Then along came Jackie Robinson. At the time, Aaron told his father that he would one day play against Robinson. They hardly encouraged such fanciful and dangerous dreams. James Baldwin, who grew up in Harlem in the early part of the century, speaks to such parental concern: "The fear that I heard in my father's voice, for example, when he realized that I really *believed* I could do anything a white boy could do, and had every intention of proving it, was not at all like the fear I heard when one of us was ill or fallen down the stairs or strayed too far from the house. It was another fear, a fear that the child, in challenging the white world's assumptions, was putting himself in the path of destruction."[46]

Scott made three trips to the Aaron household only to be told each time that Henry wasn't there.

About a week after his third visit, "I'm at the park, shagging some balls in center field myself, getting ready for the game. I look up and see somebody coming to the gate. With him was his daddy and I run got a suit on him. I wanted to see him play."[47]

While nothing so storied as Henry belting a tape-measure home run with his first swing at his first at bat happened, Scott says that he did "like to tore the fence down. You could hear it rattle for six blocks."[48]

Not long after, Scott signed Aaron to play for Indianapolis. From there he was sold to the Boston Braves and rose quickly through their farm system, debuting with the parent club, moved to Milwaukee, on April 13, 1954.

Ed Scott took a picture of young Henry standing beside the railroad tracks, waiting to board the train for Indianapolis, the first time he would leave Mobile. Henry has his hands folded behind his back. He's wearing a long-sleeved dress shirt buttoned at the collar, pressed trousers, and black wingtip shoes. There is a look of both uncertainty and determination on his face. At his feet is a small cloth bag containing his baseball glove with a ball tucked inside and, he has said famously, "two pants, two dollars, and two sandwiches." Twenty-two years later that young boy in the laundered pants and shirt, without a single wrinkle on his fresh, smooth face, and only the tiniest hint of fear in his eyes, would break Babe Ruth's career home run record, a record many said would never be broken, that had lasted for generations, a record Aaron still owns to this day.

Aaron suffered through unimaginable racial abuse as he approached Ruth's record, a full decade *after* King's imploring speech. And Jackie died shortly before the feat was fully realized, the fall before the 1973 season, when it became evident that the only thing that might keep Aaron from breaking the record would be some rabid fan following through on the multitude of death threats he received. But Robinson is the first one Aaron credits for his momentous success, as the example of serenity to see his way through such difficult times, and as the man who opened the door for even the possibility of success.

In the spring of 1954, the Dodgers again made a barnstorming trip through Mobile, Alabama. This time, the team they played their exhibition game against was the Milwaukee Braves, with newly promoted twenty-year-old Henry Aaron in the lineup.

Henry's prediction that he would play against Robinson one day came to pass. What's more, it happened in his hometown, at Hartwell Field—not far from where he whiled away countless summer days launching bottle caps and softballs and baseballs and bound strips of old cloth high and deep into the tropical air, dreaming dreams just as lofty and far-reaching—with those once-fearful parents, now bursting with pride, in attendance.

Henry's place on the Braves roster was made possible by the kind of event that makes you think about the sanctifying quality of Mobile's water, the grip of providence, the power of belief. In February of that year, 1954, the Giants traded Bobby Thomson—he of "the shot heard 'round the world"—to the Milwaukee Braves, a move that was, Kahn says, "defiant of decent sentiment."[49]

A month later, during the earliest stages of spring training for the new season, running the bases in a Braves uniform, Thomson broke his ankle sliding into third base. The player they called up from their farm club in Eau Claire, Wisconsin, to fill Thomson's spot on the roster was Henry Aaron. From a vantage point more than fifty years later, the event might seem like a common enough occurrence, one of the inherent vagaries of any athletic endeavor. With the odds at the time so great against even someone as talented as Henry Aaron, though, it takes on something of a broader significance. This was still two months before

the Supreme Court's decision on *Brown v. Board of
Education*, the class-action suit brought on behalf of
all black public school children in America that had
been slowly making its way through the courts since
1951. The reason Henry was playing softball when
Scott discovered him was because the segregated high
school he attended, Central High School, didn't have
a baseball team, didn't have much of any kind of athletic department. The *Brown* decision rests on the
Court's belief that "In these days, it is doubtful that
any child may reasonably be expected to succeed in
life if he is denied the opportunity of an education."[50]

On the dark side of the veil, opportunity was
something only whispered about in hushed tones,
something rare and elusive and precious, something
spoken of with the kind of reverence that you can
only hope for a chance to witness some day, like
seeing Jackie Robinson in his crisp Brooklyn Dodgers
baseball uniform playing professional major league
baseball. For other American children, even immi-
grant children, like Bobby Thomson, opportunity was
an assumed birthright or the reason they came to
these shores in the first place, maybe even something
expected. Given such circumstances, how unreason-
able is it to wonder if Thomson's and Aaron's paths
crossing in such a manner isn't the result of a tide of
inevitability pushed into motion seven years earlier
through the collective efforts of Branch Rickey and
Jackie Robinson? Who's to say, in other words, it isn't

always, hasn't always been, in the water? Not an answer to either question, obviously, so much as something that keeps them suspended, floating on the surface, but later that season, Aaron's rookie season, which had been going well enough, Henry broke his ankle, sliding into third base, and had to finish the season on the bench, a nod to the water gods, perhaps, or the circularity of life, as symbolized by a sphere spun of threads, wrapped round and round and covered in horsehide.

By 1954, his career past its zenith, already suffering the debilitating effects of diabetes at only thirty-five years of age, Jackie Robinson knew full well it took deliberate action to bring about change. Jackie must have known by then that his agonizing about his treatment in the earliest part of the 1947 season, his hope that people would "put that together," and that they might come to realize that because a black man was a good ballplayer, a black man could be viewed as a good man, was little more than wishful thinking. The veil was stronger than that, thicker than water, or blood. "The common experience for persons of African descent living in the United States was to be caught in the grip of stereotype and assumption. The ordinary expectation of being treated as a human being—the birthright of almost any white—was impossible. The consequences of such a profound social disconnection went beyond slavery and Reconstruction to

all the miseries of contemporary racism: poverty, segregation, repression, resistance, self-deception, and
self-doubt."[51]

It took more than being allowed to play baseball,
or any other quotas, or equalizing the relative mixes
in the nation's classrooms, to lift the veil and be seen
as a good ballplayer, a good man, a human being. But
Jackie had shown, by the waning months of that first
season, through baseball and his deliberate actions on
the field, that obstacles could be broken down and,
with difficulty, progress could be made.

In the sixth inning of a game in 1947, on August
29, the first game of a three-game series against the
Giants in Brooklyn, with the pennant on the line,
Jackie, on the base path, showed what it would take.

Falkner writes, "shoehorned into the ballpark
were 34,512 fans screaming, banging cowbells,
stomping their feet. Jackie Robinson, the major
leagues' first black player in the twentieth century,
was on third base, dancing back and forth, threatening to steal home. Who could measure the dreams
of those who watched him: all those fans; the gallery
of writers hung from the upper deck; the executives,
including Branch Rickey; the thirty-six-year-old vet-
eran pitcher, Joe Beggs?"

Jackie took off on the next pitch, but stopped
short—nobody could stop shorter, Kahn writes—
"stopped as though within the engine of his body he
possessed an unknown gear that could throw all of his

two hundred forward-hurtling pounds instantly into nimble-footed retreat. He was back at third, his hands on his hips, before the startled catcher, Walker Cooper, could make up his mind to throw either to third or back to the mound."[52]

Jackie had merely been calculating the time it took the pitcher to get the ball to the plate from the exact point on the base path where he stopped. On the next pitch, to a wave of concussive crowd noise, Jackie took off again, "flying on pigeon-toed, spindly legs, arms flopping, his head a bauble above the dust as he slid beneath the tag applied by Walker Cooper." Safe. "For the third time in this epochal opening season of his, he had stolen home, had dismantled that invisible barrier confronting base runners of any size, shape, or color standing at third base; he had dismantled it as he had only months before dismantled a century of bigotry that had seemingly permanently sealed America's Pastime."[53]

Rickey's "noble experiment."

During spring training of the year Henry Aaron would be discovered swatting fast-pitch softballs, 1952, the Dodgers were grooming another young black man for baseball stardom, rookie pitcher Joe Black. They bunked him in with Robinson at their training facilities in Florida, hoping some of Jackie's "competitiveness" would rub off on him. The day they settled in, after Jackie showed him where linens and other supplies were located, he asked Black how big he was, said, "You can fight too, can't you?" Black answered, "I sure can."

"He looked at me—and I'll always remember that look—and he says, 'But we're not gonna fight.' I didn't know what he meant, so I asked him. He tells me that they're gonna be calling us names, wherever we go, whatever we do. I was surprised by that because it was like five years after, right, and everybody said the bad stuff was in the past. No, Jackie said, 'They're gonna call you names and they're gonna do something, you won't know what exactly, but it will be something—and we're not gonna fight.' He said it just like that. He said, 'That's what they want us to do. And we're going to ignore them.' I'll never forget his talking to me like that."[54]

Jackie was speaking from experience, of course, but he also understood the struggle would be long and grueling, would require constant vigilance and control. He knew the greater significance of Rickey's experiment. He knew the importance of his success and was capable of taking on a leadership role in that fight, all fights, in the clubhouse, on the field, in the world. For a five-year span starting in 1949, the year he won the league's Most Valuable Player award, being both batting champion and stolen-base leader, Robinson was at the top of his game, a perennial leader in several offensive and fielding categories, placing him among a handful of the greatest in the game. He led by his performance and his competitive intensity and his outspokenness. "Jackie Robinson knew that as this team flourished, so went that very fragile flower of opportunity that had been inching up from the ground. No matter how he had been crowded, compromised, and limited, the struggle was on the field—exactly where Jackie Robinson was surest about what he could give."[55]

And it was during spring training in 1954, before Bobby Thomson broke his ankle and Henry Aaron was promoted, that Robinson made a phone call to another black player dismantling a color barrier. Not another major leaguer, though there were plenty of teams that had yet to integrate, and not even a player somewhere else in the Dodger system. He called Nat Peeples, the first and only black player in the old Southern Association, the league that the Mobile Bears had won back in 1947. Robinson phoned him shortly after he'd been signed by the Atlanta Crackers, a move that threatened to bring a ruinous boycott against the team's ownership company, Coca-Cola, as racism was so entrenched, even officially endorsed, in Georgia.

"He told me my job would be harder than his," Peeples said. "We talked for a while. He told me what he had been through and what I could expect. Most important, he said, was to keep a level head. They'll call me anything and everything and I had to turn a deaf ear to it."[56]

*

Robinson knew from direct experience how especially difficult it was going to be for Peeples. He is credited with integrating Atlanta sports when he played three exhibition games there as a Dodger back in 1949, despite published threats from the Grand Kleagle of the Klan himself, Dr. Samuel Green, as well as against Atlanta's baseball Crackers. The Southern Association was one of the last minor leagues to integrate when Peeples debuted on April 9, 1954, as a pinch-hitter in a game against the Bears at Mobile's Hartwell Field, four days before Henry Aaron debuted as the last player "drafted" out of the Negro Leagues, his contract bought in the middle of 1952 by the Braves. Aaron would find Atlanta could still be inhospitable and threatening twenty years later when he was on the cusp of becoming the greatest home run hitter of all time.

Jackie's example showed both Peeples and Aaron, and countless other black players, that their personal indignation was a secondary matter. That "fragile flower of opportunity" was their charge, their responsibility, for that fight wasn't near over. In a lot of respects, he knew, it was just beginning, even as his days as a ballplayer were dwindling.

In 1955 the great Dodger team designed primarily by Branch Rickey years earlier finally won Brooklyn's lone championship, beating the hated Yankees after falling to them so many other times in the World Series during the Robinson era. By then most everyone in baseball understood that Jackie's skills were diminishing, his weight unchecked, his legs shot. But in the eighth inning of the first game, with the Yankees leading 6 to 3, Jackie set the tone for what would be a hard -fought seven-game series. With one out and one runner on, he bounced a grounder off third-baseman Gil McDougal's knee, reaching second on the error, as Carl Furillo, the runner, advanced to third. A sacrifice fly scored Furillo, and Jackie, defying conventional baseball wisdom, moved to third with two outs.

On the mound for the Yankees was the great Whitey Ford. Jackie, old and heavy, still danced off the bag, the crowd of 63,869 at the old Yankee Stadium squirming in anticipation. On Ford's second pitch, Robinson broke for the plate, hurtling down the line keeping pace with the baseball, destined to converge at the plate—"the harmony of mayhem," Falkner called it. A perfect slide, hooking away from Yogi Berra, saw Robinson, the creator of opportunities, called safe at home, over the protests of Berra.

"Mr. Jesse talked to us about opportunity," Ellis May says quietly.

Pugh nods his head, mutters, "Mmm-hmm."

"He talked about opportunities on the ball field *all* the time," Candyman continues.

Madison takes up the call and response, "That's

right."

"But he also talked to us about opportunities in *life*."

When Robinson was their age, growing up in Pasadena, California—even if, by comparison to these Mohawks, he was not confronted with the same entrenched obstacles—the "overriding reality" of his early years was that, "for black youth, the future was closed. Simple as that."[57]

Things were different enough by the 1950s, thanks to Jackie Robinson, that Jesse Norwood's lesson to his Mohawks was tinged with more promise and optimism, though he was still fully aware of the realities. The future for those black youth was still relatively closed, not to say threatened. Emmett Till, the same age as some of them when it happened, had been murdered in the summer of 1955 in Mississippi for daring to address a white woman. Closer to home that spring, Claudette Colvin, a sixteen-year-old high school student, was arrested for not yielding her seat on a Montgomery bus, the case initially used to test Alabama's segregation laws six months before Rosa Parks did. What Mr. Jesse taught them to focus on was the example of Jackie Robinson, an example that those closed doors would some day open.

"My father always used to say," Jesse Norwood, Jr., speaks up, "that the door would swing open some day, but it wouldn't stay open. 'Your job,' he would say, 'our *job*, was to be ready when it did, ready to stick our foot in the door and hold it open, for as long as we could, so that we, and however many others we can drag along with us, could get through the door."

James "Popcorn" Campbell stands in the back of the room with his head bowed. Others, Madison, Emanuel, Pugh, simply nod. Not Candyman. He sits staring straight ahead, "dead red," as he calls it, and says, "Yes sir, that's what he said. And that's what we did, what we're doing today."

Five

"You want to know about Mr. Jesse Norwood?" Candyman asks after some silence. "I'll tell you about Mr. Jesse Norwood."

He leans back in his chair, rubs at his chin, says, "We played a game in Jackson, Mississippi, once. What year was that fellas?"

The others only laugh at the memory May is poised to summon.

Pugh asks, "1958?"

After some more thought, May says, "Naw. Had to be '59." He narrows his eyes and looks around the room. He has penetrating, searching brown eyes. "It was the year Theodore came to the team," he says motioning to Sellers behind him.

"Theodore could *bring* it," Pugh says.

"Yes, sir, we was getting good by that time. We had developed some skills, our strength," May adds, flexing an arm. "We started attracting those good ballplayers to *our* team. Samuel Coates," he says, holding up a finger.

"Old Sam-yule," Madison echoes, nodding his

head. "Ol' Lank."

"You was already with the team, right, Sam?" Ellis says, still narrowing it down. "It was the year Robert Weaver came over. He was a *nasty* knuckleballer," he says, and shudders. "Had to be '59."

"We rolled into Jackson, Mississippi, in our station wagons, with our mothers and friends and neighbors, complete with a police escort," May says with a gleam in those eyes, raising his hands like he's testifying to Jesus. "Yes sir, we were a thing by that time, the Prichard Mohawks."

"We had our jackets on," Madison says, tugging at the lapels of his shirt, "and everything."

Team jackets. Black satin with the team logo. The players all say they wore those jackets everywhere, speaking of the garments with as much fondness as anything else about the time.

"And everywhere we went, people would call out, 'Look, there go the Mohawks!'" Madison says, pointing. "Oh, we looked *good* in those jackets."

Sam's comment brings a big smile to Campbell's face, as he stands there, rubbing his hands together, like he's scuffing up a baseball, readying to pitch.

"Now Jackson, Mississippi, in nineteen fifty-nine is not a real friendly place," Candyman continues.

"Especially," Pugh drawls, "when you're playing a white team."

"Lily-white," Candyman says.

"The local favorites," Madison adds.

"And we was *all* black. Not the friendliest place at *all*," May says.

"No, sir," Pugh says.

"But things was okay. They gave us our money, for playing. Gave us some sandwiches. And then we got around to the baseball."

"Oh, boy," Pugh grumbles.

"We scored five runs in the first inning," Candyman says, the fingers of his right hand splayed to show the count. "Ol' Lyonel here had himself a three-run homer."

Pugh sits there bobbing his head slightly, like it's no big deal. Everything about Lyonel Pugh is languid, and smooth. He wears a light blue fleece warm-up suit. He has an easy smile, though a little self-conscious, from a missing tooth. He likes to laugh, but nothing boisterous, a sound easy and fluid, athletic. He is an athlete. The overriding sense is that he would really rather just play ball more than anything else, more than talk, certainly.

"Yes sir, rang up five counts in our first at bat. But guess who's the umpire? That *same* sheriff who'd come to greet us," May continues. "When we take the field in the bottom of the inning, Mr. Sellers here, who usually had pretty good control, well he can't *buy* himself a strike."

"The zone just shrank away to nothing," Sellers says, shaking his head. "Everything was a ball."

"And then," Madison adds, "everything *they*

threw up there was a strike! Everything. Didn't matter if it bounced two times to the plate."

"Had us swinging at balls clear over our heads," little Bennie Harris says.

"Pretty soon it's 5 to 3, and we can't hardly do anything about it." May says. "Well, after five innings of this stuff Mr. Jesse hollers from the dugout, 'All right, fellas, that's enough! I ain't taking no more. Candyman' he yells to me, in that same booming voice, though I'm sitting right next to him. 'Get the stuff together. Let's go.'

"'bout this time the sheriff comes out and says, 'Hold it! Where you going?'

"Jesse said, 'Going *home*.'

"Sheriff said, 'No you're not. Y'all gonna play this ball game.'

"Mr. Jesse said, 'Can't play.'

"'You gonna play.'

"'We *can't* play,' Mr. Jesse said again. 'We came here to play baseball. This isn't baseball,' he says, nose-to-nose with Mr. Sheriff, his arms crossed, not budging one damn bit.

"Well, sir, we got us a standoff, is what we got," May says, settling back in his chair, arms folded just like his mentor.

"A *stand*off," Pugh echoes.

Candyman plays the crowd.

"Somebody called in more sheriffs, gonna *quell* this disturbance."

Harris covers his mouth.

"Still, Mr. Jesse doesn't even blink."

"No, sir," Madison sings out.

"Before we knew it, they had *ten* patrol cars at the ballpark," Candyman says, thrusting both hands before him, "Had us *surrounded*! We're thinking, Oh Lord, we're going to jail."

Campbell turns his back on the scene, his shoulders quaking. Even the reserved Lomax is finding it hard not to join in. Jesse Norwood Jr. stands beside him, grinning from both amusement and pride, at this picture of his father.

"And Mr. Jesse Norwood did not budge one, damn, inch," May says, jabbing the tip of one finger into the tabletop. "He said, 'I don't give a damn if I do go to jail. You're going to start calling these balls right or we're going home. Stop cheating my boys!'"

"We wasn't nothing but boys," Candyman says. "He made that sheriff back down. *Made* him call a fair game. And we beat them fellas, 10 to 4!"

"Whooped 'em," Madison calls.

"*That's* Mr. Jesse Norwood," May says, slapping the table. "*That's* the man we're talking about."

That man's son leads the room in spontaneous applause after Candyman's story, May sitting stern, and serious, and full of righteous conviction.

"But," Pugh mumbles, in the aftermath of the applause, and the laughter, "we was scared to *death* all the way out of Mississippi going home that night."

That cracks Candyman's composure, sends the

room into a renewed fit of laughing and crying out.

The men settle down again eventually, shaking their heads, some wiping tears from the corners of their eyes.

"Mr. Jesse sure took care of us," one of them says, to the murmured agreement of others.

"Made it so we didn't ever want to quit the Mohawks," May says.

"Candyman came back from the army to play ball," Pugh tells me.

"I took one at bat," Ellis reminds him.

Lyonel chuckles, remembering. "Tell him *that* story."

Candyman thinks for a moment and says, "Naw. That ain't no baseball story. We're here to talk *baseball*. "Why don't you tell him *your* story?"

"You the talker."

"I'm *tired* of talking."

"Better do as he says, Lyonel," Madison tells him. "Or he'll throw you off the team again."

"You and me *both*," Emanuel adds.

May answers, "I just might," which brings another round of laughter.

"Yes, sir, Mr. *President*," Pugh says again, though he's clearly yielding, sitting up straighter, ready to start the story. "I'll tell *that* story."

But it's Emanuel who pipes up, saying, "Threw the two of us off the team for 'trying to take over,' he said."

"I was the boss!"

"Took our uniforms away."

"Yup, that's right," Pugh says. "Took our jackets too."

"They didn't pay their fines."

"We was only doing what Mr. Jesse would have done," Pugh offers, though there's a still of hint of contrition in his voice nearly half a century later.

"You know that don't cut nothing, Lyonel," Madison tells him. "You remember the time Candyman threw Mr. Jesse out of a meeting, don't you?"

"Yup, mmm-hmm. I sure do."

"Just doing what it said in the book," May says, not apologizing to anyone.

Mr. Jesse had given Ellis "the book," *Robert's Rules of Order*, around the time of their adventure in Jackson in 1958, or '59, when he'd appointed May the team president. By that time May had moved from position to position, from shortstop to third base, to the outfield, only to be supplanted by other, more talented players. It didn't help May that he couldn't bring himself to stand in at the plate against breaking stuff.

"I was *scared* of curveballs," he admits, to some needling from the others.

He had migrated to the bench where Jesse approached him one day and said, "Candyman, we need a team president." Pugh had replaced May at third base. And when they recruited Madison, he took Candyman's position in left field. Ellis says he was sitting on the bench, "feeling *rejected*, feeling *forgotten*," when Mr. Jesse came over and reminded him, "*Every-body's* got a job. We need us a team president."

He gave him the 1951, seventy-fifth anniversary edition, *Robert's Rules Newly Revised*, told him to study it, then put him in charge of the scorebook during the games and set him up as a parliamentarian governing their meetings. During those meetings, then, Mr. Jesse would sit off to the side while the team conducted their business. One night, so the story goes, Mr. Jesse was offering comments as the boys debated one motion or another.

"Chief," Ellis told him, "I'm going to have to ask you to leave the room if you don't stop interrupting."

"But this is my team," Mr. Jesse told him.

"And you made me the boss."

"It's still my team!"

"I did the only thing I could do," Candyman says.

"He put Mr. Jesse out of the room."

"What it says in the book," May answers.

The affair with Emanuel and Pugh was no less cut and dried, at least in Candyman's eyes. They had been fined by the team—according to long-established bylaws—for arguing with an umpire.

"And they didn't pay their fines," he says.

"We was *only* doing what Mr. Jesse would have done."

"They didn't pay their fines," May repeats.

"He put us off the team," Pugh laments.

"Took away our uniforms."

"Our *jackets*!"

"Until they paid their fines," May says, unrelenting, but then can't resist adding, "and begged back on."

"We voted *him* out as president the next year."

"Like it says in the book," May concedes. They voted him back in the following year, however. "Because I'm a natural organizer," he says, flashing that Candyman smile.

The book, originally published in 1876, was created by Henry Martyn Robert, an engineering officer in the army. He was asked to preside over a church meeting and didn't know how. The embarrassing experience of trying to operate without any guidelines for protocol brought him to the determination *never* to attend another such meeting until he knew something about parliamentary procedure.

He discovered very few books on the subject, and in his travels as a military man he found virtual parliamentary chaos wherever he went, since everyone seemed to have differing ideas of correct procedure. The original title was *Pocket Manual of Rules of Order for Deliberative Assemblies*, and it came to be called *Robert's Rules of Order*. It has been through ten editions now, each revised by either Robert, a relative, or someone who worked on a previous edition.

It was in 1860s San Francisco that Robert encountered a society "out of order." This was a society culled from every part of the globe and all points of the political spectrum. Represented in that society

were the original adventurers who had first "discovered" the territory, the remnants of native inhabitants,
Asian, Mexican, and Spanish immigrants, midwestern
homesteaders, eastern speculators, white separatists,
and black refugees. It was the period immediately
after the society at large had suffered through the
most extreme example of a society out of order, the
Civil War. Recognizing the need for, and realizing the
only hope for, any kind of harmony among all those
divergent groups, Robert set about studying parliamentary procedure and law, first developed in Great
Britain and necessarily adapted by Thomas Jefferson
and the founding fathers.

Jefferson's appreciation of the Iroquois democratic
society, which would find its way into his manual on
constitutional governance—the ready reference Robert
used to outline his rules of parliamentary procedure
for *any* deliberative assembly—may have been what
prompted Jesse Norwood to insist Ellis May rely on
Robert's Rules of Order in his capacity as president of
the team, though no one can say for sure. It is hard to
imagine that there was ever a point in his hard-
scrabble life when he would have felt like he'd benefited at all from any so-called ordered society. But
maybe his understanding of the *theory* employed—
wherever he might have encountered it—was enough
to sustain a belief that the system, theoretically, was
the best hope for a fair and ordered representative
society, just as his understanding of the *theory* of base-

ball (however he acquired *that* knowledge) was enough to sustain the conviction that the beneficial effects of the game reached far beyond the playing field. The world he operated within in 1959 was still a few years removed from a time when the United States legislature would pass the Voting Rights Act. That act might serve as an example of how the model reflected in *Robert's Rules* did indeed work (that is, because of parliamentary law, the body was able to overcome resistance from a rogue contingent of Dixie democrats), but in Norwood's society, two years later, voter registration workers would still be murdered for trying to effect the law. Mr. Jesse could *only* have realized the merits of the system as it was set down in a book somewhere, those who knew him best said.

"He picked it up in some book, I'm sure," his widow, Hattie, said, twenty years after Norwood's passing. "He had all kinds of books."

At the time, 1993, not long before she too would pass, she sat on a stool in the back porch of the home where they'd raised their children, on Bullshead Avenue in Prichard, Alabama, trimming the tops of fresh, tender okra pods from a bushel basket at her feet. She would boil the okra, along with peas and ham hocks, for her church supper later in the day. For the time being, she sat patiently answering questions about her husband, selecting another piece of okra from the basket, slicing off the stem with a black-handled paring knife guided against the calloused thumb of her right hand and placing it into another bowl. A slightly unbalanced ceiling fan droned overhead, slowly stirring the thick air. It was a spring Sunday afternoon, baseball time, though the games, and teams like the Mohawks, were long gone. The Trinity Gardens Recreational facilities were just a hope. The day was hot, and heavy, with thunder clouds massing in the south that would rumble in and dump a load of rain on the city by evening. Another fan, a white oscillating one, sat on the porch planking at Hattie's feet, sweeping back and forth, cooling the woman at her task. "It was the rain," Hattie said, reminded by the rumblings outside. The rain over the years beat down and leaked into the old clubhouse out back and ruined the scorebooks and records of the Mohawk games. She "burned 'em," she said. Her eldest child, son Melvin, came in the back door just then, after searching for any surviving logs or books.

"It's a funny thing," he said of the missing items. He thought he'd seen them recently, though he couldn't say where, or when. "A funny, funny thing."

He remembered the books, and the meetings, and the caravans to games. Asked if he played, he smiled, shook his head and said, "No, no, I couldn't play. I wasn't first string stuff." Then he said, "I played one game. Right field. I went running back for a fly ball." Jumping up and turning back toward the door there on the porch, Melvin said, "Hit my head against the wall," rubbing at the spot thirty years later. "I *sure* wanted one of those jackets they wore, though."

Hattie paused in her work, knife in one hand, okra in the other. "You should have *seen* those boys in them jackets. Oh, but they sure looked pretty," she said, shaking her head, resuming.

Melvin talked about the peanut roasts in the Norwood kitchen, roasting hundred-pound sacks of raw peanuts and divvying the cooked peanuts out into little paper sacks that would be distributed to the players and sold on street corners, after church services and at football games. He talked about his father buying supplies for the team, even though they had to work, selling peanuts, mowing lawns, running errands, to help pay off his "notes." That taught them to take responsibility for the enterprise, even as he was taking on the responsibility for their lives, something he would continue to do for the rest of his life.

"If any of the players ever got picked up—" Melvin started.

His mother interrupted, "Those boys never caused any trouble!"

"No, oh no," Melvin agreed. "But they still got *picked* up. The funny thing is, those police would always call Dad instead of any parents."

Melvin quieted down and stared into a private space. "Knock on wood," he said, reaching down and rapping his knuckles against the chair leg beneath him. "No one will be saying anything bad about my dad." Then he smiled again, whether from some private joke or some memory of his father, he never revealed, saying only, "It's a funny, funny thing."

Sam Madison grows stern and speaks to that: "There ain't no bad things to be said about Mr. Jesse. He didn't *believe* in 'bad' boys. He always used to say, 'Bo, you just wasn't in the right place at the right time.' He called me Bo."

Madison bows his head. The others stay silent, allowing him this moment. They know his story.

Quiet, easy Lyonel Pugh breaks the silence, asking, "Do y'all remember ol' 'Left-eye'?"

"Adam Shut," May says. "Now that was a *bad* man."

"Not to Mr. Jesse," Madison insists. "He changed *his* life too."

Norwood recruited Shut to run his concession stand at Mohawk Park for the Sunday evening doubleheaders.

"'Cause he was good at holding money," Pugh says, chuckling.

"We all thought he would rob us blind. He was a bad, *bad* man," May says.

"Not to Mr. Jesse," Madison repeats. "He said, 'Left-eye, I'm making you responsible for these proceeds. If there's anything out of order, I'm coming to you,' he told him, di-rectly," Madison says.

"Dead red," Candyman chants.

Pugh, still tickled by the situation, says, "Ol' Left-eye sure did take care of Mr. Jesse's *proceeds*."

"Rehabilitated a bad man, right on the spot," Madison finishes, talking directly to Pugh.

May pulls himself up straighter in his chair, braces one forearm on the tabletop and raises his right hand, index finger extended. "That does *not* mean, though," he says, looking at the faces around him, "That he couldn't be put out of a meeting for being bad himself, according to *Robert's Rules of Order*."

Campbell, the last face Candyman lights upon, still standing in the back of the room, just rolls his eyes for his former president.

"It's true," Candyman insists.

Mr. Jesse could be expelled from a meeting of his team in a clubhouse he built on his property: it is true.

"Says so right in the book!"

"I'm surprised you don't still have that book," Emanuel says to May.

"Mr. President," Pugh adds.

Ellis May studied the book, as he was told, and didn't need to keep possession of it, really, he came to know it so well. Page 299:

"Every deliberative assembly has the right to decide who may be present during its session; and when the assembly, either by a rule or by a vote, decides that a certain person shall not remain in the room, it is the duty of the chairman to enforce the rule of order, using whatever force is necessary to eject the party."[58]

*

"It was my duty," Candyman says.

"Right."

It is just as likely, though, Mr. Norwood was trying to show them the strength of the system, that the system established by Jefferson and those others, despite the circumstances of his life, and their lives, could indeed work. They all knew those circumstances. Mr. Jesse told them that too. They knew that in wider spheres they were all but invisible boys, and in the vernacular of Ralph Ellison's novel published in 1952, would probably grow to be invisible men, with invisible children of their own. In the smaller arena of their organization, within the workings of their team, the Mohawks, they would operate according to the ideals of representative, parliamentary governance. That was the only way the ideal could spread to wider and wider applications. He wanted to be sure they recognized and understood it, for that was part of being ready for those doors of opportunity opening. They must, in fact, realize that the ideal of just and equal representation was the force prying open what few doors would crack in their lifetimes, allowing them to get through and to pull however many others through with them. In 1950s Prichard, Alabama, Jesse Norwood had no reason to expect or hope for fair and just deliberative treatment within the society at large. On the contrary, the design of a Jim Crow society specifically suppressed the will of its minorities. It would take time, and acts of Congress, to convince that society that such minorities as Jesse Norwood and his band of Mohawks could lay claim to equal representation, that they even possessed a voice. There is no reason they could even conceive of such a society at the time, except for Jesse Norwood and their team, modeled after the best of baseball organizations, governed by democratic ideals. With the experience and knowledge of how democratic representative societies were *supposed* to work, they could really be ready to step through that resistant door of opportunity. "Understand," he was telling them, "how the system *should* work." Understand, too, how prejudice works. *Only* through such understanding could they overcome it and find those doors. "Take your own blue ink pen to fill out job applications" was one of those lessons they remember. If they didn't take their own pen, they'd be given a black pen, and in that subtle manner, marked as black men. They couldn't fight the practice, but they could defeat its effects, with understanding and preparation, just like on the ball field, creating opportunities through readiness. Like it or not, that was the circumstance of their lives, what they would continually encounter, what their children would probably encounter, even on ball fields beyond the order of their own. And they can all tell stories today which testify to that.

"Tell him your story, Pugh," Candyman urges his friend again.

Late in the 1960 season, Lyonel Pugh was signed

to a professional baseball contract with the Philadelphia Phillies.

"Signed by Buck O'Neil," Pugh says. "A legend."

"*And* a black man," Madison adds.

Pugh was a tall, loose-limbed young man. He played either position on the left side of the infield, quick with his glove, as quick on his feet. He was, at the time, one of the earliest examples of what would become the modern prototype for shortstops and third basemen, the antecedent of someone like Alex Rodriguez, the greatest all-around player of our generation. Along with his partner in crime, Emanuel, Pugh was one of the fastest players on the Mohawks team, and speed was an increasingly important component of the team's game. They relied on speed and aggressiveness at a time when the big-league model was something more like a chess match, as George Will characterizes it: get a man on base and wait for home run lightning. When Maury Wills set the stolen-base record at 104 in 1962, Leonard Koppett considered that a greater, more significant accomplishment than Maris eclipsing Ruth's home run record a year earlier. Jesse Norwood understood that somehow nearly a full decade before.

"We ran *all* the time," Pugh says. "*All* the time."

There were nine black ballplayers attending Philadelphia's camp that next spring, at a time when segregation was still the rule in the South. Just the previous winter, in Greensboro, North Carolina, four black college freshmen sat down at a Woolworth's lunch counter. There they remained, unserved, until closing time. Others would follow, and suffer for it. They would be arrested, ridiculed; they would have salt or sugar poured on them by white bystanders. The situation was much the same at Philadelphia's training site in Florida. The black ballplayers were put up in private houses in the black sections of town, whereas the rest of the team stayed in hotels and had catered meals. Not much had changed in all the years since Jackie Robinson accompanied the Dodger organization to Florida in 1946. Among the nine black players in 1960 was Richie Allen, and among the things that hadn't changed, was the unspoken quota system that had been in place ever since 1946, the same system Bill Dillard recognized in Jasmine, Mississippi, in 1957 when he was trying out for San Francisco alongside Willie McCovey; the same system even Branch Rickey alluded to back in 1950 when he is said to have felt, after signing Robinson and New-combe and Campanella, that three black players on any major league team were enough, were as much as the larger society of white spectators would tolerate. Competing for a position against a future rookie of the year and MVP—not against the whole of the organization's prospects—Pugh was still good enough to have a rookie baseball card made, and signed, and distributed in those packs of cards with that stick of bubblegum. But he didn't stay in Florida. Whether he was unable to bear up under the conditions of Jim Crow, or whether he yielded to the pressures of superior baseball skills, he won't say, but he returned to Prichard, returned to the Mohawks.

"Just came home," is all he says. He sits in his chair, staring down at his hands. He smiles to himself at what happened next.

The next year he signed with another big-league organization, the San Francisco Giants. He played on their rookie team for a month outside of Roanoke, Virginia, until they found out about his Philadelphia rookie card. For reasons he never fully understood, or had explained, that made him ineligible, and they let him go, back to Prichard, back to the Mohawks.

"You just wasn't in the right place at the right time," his longtime friend Sam Madison tells him, echoing Jesse Norwood.

"Just like John Lee," Bennie Harris chimes in.

Cowan, his partner, was another Mohawk recruited and signed by major league scouts. He went off to play in the Carolina bus leagues but didn't stay the whole season. When he showed up back in Prichard, he only told them he was homesick, homesick for their ballpark there in Trinity Gardens, for the Mohawks.

"Not the right place at the right time," Harris agrees, looking over his shoulder at Sam.

"But it was," Pugh answers, raising his head, nodding it, his eyes bright, almost amused by it all, showing no trace of bitterness. "It was home."

Mohawk Park was the right place for these men because it was home, more of a home, for some of them, than they'd otherwise experienced in their lives, just as Jesse Norwood was more of a father than they'd previously known, and their baseball team was more of a family than they could find anywhere else. Compared to where they'd come from and what they encountered outside of Prichard, Mohawk Park was paradise.

Not surprisingly, A. Bartlett Giamatti would point out some years later that the root of the word "paradise" is an ancient Persian word meaning "enclosed park or green." Places like Mohawk Park existed, he told us, because there is in our core, our human core, "a vestigial memory of an enclosed green space as a place of freedom and play."[59]

The contrast between that home in Trinity Gardens, Alabama, and ballparks in Miami, Florida, or Roanoke, Virginia, or Durham, North Carolina, was unbearable. While the segregationists in those towns might tolerate a black ballplayer having his two or three hours of playing time several days a week, they imprisoned his humanity within the limits of those ball fields, veiling him with epithets and invective from as near as the first row of seats. And outside of that confinement, that same ballplayer was merely another member of an inferior and subservient race in their eyes, someone relegated to that other water fountain, the outhouse removed from any public establishment, someone who had to vacate any sidewalk he found himself sharing with a white citizen. Why wouldn't they want to come home to a ballpark they were free to enter or exit through any available portal, where they could play against and alongside white ballplayers without their lives being threatened, where their presence on the street, in their Mohawk jackets, was a cause for celebration, and pride?

But for any of those Mohawks willing to run the gauntlet of racial intolerance in those other Southern towns, a stranger in the all-too-familiar land of Jim Crow, in an effort to further their baseball skills and rise through the professional ranks, Mohawk Park was the right place to be if they wanted to get scouted. There were five or six big-league scouts at every game, they say. Most of the players in the room generated interest from those scouts, and many of them signed contracts, though the lure of the home team, of playing for Jesse Norwood and the Mohawks, was too strong. It's as Dillard says, for most of them: "Once I got on the Mohawks, I didn't want to play anywhere else."

"*Everyone* wanted to be a Mohawk," May says.

"It's true," says Dr. Jimmy Knight. He's an educator, an administrator with the Mobile County Board of Education, in the largest school district in the state. He worries about today's kids, about who's going to step into the shoes of the Jesse Norwoods, Jesse Thomases, and James Richardsons to lead this generation. But of that time, he says that in his travels with the Royals and the Giants, whenever anyone found out he was from Mobile, they'd ask him about playing for the Mohawks, how they could get up a game with the Mohawks.

"Cleon Jones wanted to be a Mohawk," Emanuel says, of the Miracle Mets' star. "But he couldn't make the team!"

Campbell, from the back of the room, thunders, "That ain't true."

"Yeah it is," Madison tells him.

Campbell shakes his head.

"Now how would you know, Popcorn?" Pugh, Campbell's early mentor, speaks up. "You was just a little bitty baby."

The others start to laughing again, before Candyman interrupts, "Gentlemen? Do we need to get out the gloves?"

Boxing gloves. That was how Mr. Jesse had them resolve disputes that couldn't be handled in any more diplomatic fashion. He pulled two pairs of gloves off the wall and had the two disputants go out into the yard and "work it out." Then they could come back to the meeting.

"Ol' Lyonel put 'em on a few times," May says.

Pugh just jabs an open left hand in his direction, waving off the subject.

Eventually, the scouts recognized the value and the strength of the Mohawks as a team, and they started bringing their prized prospects, white and black, to Ruth and First Street to play against Nor-wood's team, as a way to measure a player's ability.

Most of the ballplayers in this room nod, with a proud look in their eyes, at hearing that fact recounted.

Except Madison. He knows about wrong places and wrong times. It took most of his life to learn the value of Mr. Jesse's counter-assertion, so that now he uses it as often as he can. The early '60s saw him with a young family already, and despite the attention his home run power caught, he couldn't pursue the dream of big-league baseball. He drifted away, came back. "I couldn't find no peace," he says, and spent the next twenty-five years of his life abusing himself with alcohol for his regret at letting Mr. Jesse down, for not "making it." He wound up in rehab in 1987, fifteen years after Norwood passed, nearly dead him-self. That he came out and went on to become a long-time coach, sitting there just as proud to wear his maroon Trinity Gardens Football jacket as he was his Mohawk jacket years ago, is a testimony to his convic-tion and his strength. But he'll tell anyone who'll listen, "I wouldn't be alive today if not for Mr. Jesse Norwood."

"Making it", of course, held connotations far beyond the confines of a ball field for Jesse Norwood. "He wanted us to become good, responsible men," Reverend Robert Emanuel says from behind his desk in the offices of his church, the Friendship Baptist

Church on St. Stephens Road in Prichard, Alabama, not far from where it all started. The church has a newly painted white façade, and stout columns flank the entrance, which looks out over a neat lawn and trimmed azalea shrubbery. Inside, the light is subdued, the worship chamber quiet and empty. It's Monday afternoon, the calm after Sunday's services and before the Wednesday night prayer meeting.

When he first sat down to be interviewed, in response to an initial question about his relationship with Mr. Jesse Norwood, Reverend Emanuel paused, and then said simply, "Jesse Norwood was God."

Saying it, he peered intently before him, as if staring in from deep center field toward home plate, focused on the pitcher, the batter, ready to pick up the flight of any batted ball and chase it down.

He sits with his forearms braced atop the neat green blotter on the cleared desk, his hands folded. Behind him is a wall of glass, eight feet of ruby-tinted window, the lingering sunlight casting a deep evangelical glow over the office. Emanuel was scouted too, and recruited. He went to college instead, on a baseball scholarship, to Alabama State, a black college. There, he also ran track and studied for the seminary. He knew what he wanted to do with his life, thanks to Jesse Norwood, along with his father, and Albert Lomax, the team's coaches.

Those coaches, Emanuel Sr. and the elder Lomax, rounded out a staff modeled after any big-league operation. Emanuel was the taskmaster and disciplinarian. He was also the one who displayed his emotions most readily, charging out of the dugout to dispute a call if need be, the first to congratulate players on superb defense or stellar pitching or clutch hitting. He coached third base and was animated and mobile, windmilling his arms for a go sign, crouching down with his arms stretched in front of him signaling a stop, slapping the turf with those hands if he wanted a runner to slide. He was constantly calling out directives and encouragement. "Look alive out there, boys, look alive," he would shout, pacing beyond the coach's box, clapping his hands.

Lomax was the analyst. He studied the flow of the game, picked up quirks in a pitcher's pattern, limitations of a catcher's arm or an infielder's range. He could thoroughly dissect a game but always relayed the information to Mr. Jesse, deferring any decisions to him, the manager, who always managed in street clothes, as the great Connie Mack had.

Wearing civilian clothes meant Jesse could not enter the field of play, but he didn't have to, his son says. "He had a quiet *aura* of control," Norwood Jr. says. "He enjoyed the game and loved to watch it so much, though you couldn't hardly tell. He was not demonstrative. But if one of his *gentlemen* hit the cutoff man exactly right, or if somebody stretched a single into two bases on hustle and determination alone, you could see he was pleased."

It's quite possible that one of the books ruined by rain and then burned by Hattie Norwood was one by Connie Mack, given how Norwood's managerial style and strengths mirrored Mack's. He first published his *How to Play Base-Ball* back in 1903. And later, in 1950, Knopf published *Connie Mack's Baseball Book*. Or, more probably, Norwood had encountered a book *about* Mack, such as Frederick Lieb's *Connie Mack: Grand Old Man of Baseball*, published by Putnam in 1945. Leonard Koppett includes Mack among the "three exceptional men who not only fashioned modern baseball's development in the first half of the twentieth century but whose direct influence is still visible and ubiquitous in every ballpark" at the end of the century.[60]

Branch Rickey and John McGraw are the other two. Whether Norwood studied the man or not, there are numerous aspects of the style and method of Mack's leadership evident in Norwood's. Like Mack, Jesse Norwood was a keen judge of talent and utility. At one point he was approached by the San Francisco Giants organization to become a scout for them. He stayed with his team. He helped his "gentlemen" develop their talents with patience and instruction, in a fatherly manner, rather than demanding perfection or excellence. But he also commanded respect, with that "aura" more than anything else, so that just as the Philadelphia players always referred to their manager as Mr. Mack, the Mohawks, to a man, say they always called theirs Mr. Jesse or Mr. Norwood.

The difference, of course, is that Connie Mack was managing professional, white, major league ballplayers, men who had realized their potential and were living their dreams. Jesse Norwood was nurturing "little bitty babies" from the neighborhood, who were growing up in a world of such severe limitation that they hardly dared to dream.

"This is the story within the story," Emanuel says, his voice scratchy. He levels an index finger for emphasis. "It's one thing to have a dream. Mr. Jesse showed us how to put those dreams into action. When one *really* dreams, if you're willing to work hard enough for that dream, you'd be surprised what can come of it. That's what he taught us."

Jesse Norwood knew the odds against those boys. He'd seen Pugh go off to Miami with the Phillies in 1961, the same year President Kennedy coined the phrase "affirmative action." He knew Lyonel was a victim of a numbers crunch rather than of inadequate talent. He'd seen Ed Watts, an almost certain big-league prospect, drive off in an old car for his assignment with the Dodgers' Texas League franchise and get killed in a wreck before he ever reached Dallas. He had let them dream, even fostered some of their baseball dreams, taking them, when they were younger still, down the road to see games played by the Prichard Athletics, the area's most dominant team in the era before the Mohawks. But he also enfranchised them in their own dreams, having them earn their way into the ball park if they wanted to watch the game badly enough. He had those boys chase down balls fouled out of the park or hit beyond the outfield fence and exchange them for admission to the game.

"Making it," they were learning, sometimes meant being in the right place at the right time, as Madison says, though that's not to suggest there was merely luck involved. Something as simple as retrieving an errant baseball for a "ticket to the show" still involved anticipating where that ball would land and a willingness to work for it when it did. Luck, after all, as Branch Rickey is said to have quipped, is merely the "residue of design."[61]

The design of making it, then, depended on preparation and readiness, which meant both accepting your lot in life and working to be the best at whatever lot befell you.

"Be the best perch," Reverend Emanuel says. "If you can't be a rainbow trout, only a perch, that's all right. Be the best perch. Or it's like Dr. King said," Emanuel says, varying the imagery. "If it's your lot to be a street sweeper, be the best street sweeper, sweep that street like Michelangelo carved marble, or Beethoven composed music, or how Hank Aaron swatted a baseball, so that someone who walks by your house *knows* a street sweeper lives there. We had to do that. We had to be superior to be successful. That's the way it was in those days. We knew that; we *knew* we were baseball players, and gentlemen."

Jesse Norwood knew it too. He helped them groom their dreams, whether they were baseball or not. He helped them identify their strengths and develop them. He showed them the way to those doors of opportunity. He didn't pretend to be able to bust them down. He somehow knew that even if they couldn't all become major league baseball stars—an impossible dream—they could still become "as famous as Coke-Cola," which meant they could work to make their own success and could then turn around and influence other lives the way he'd influenced theirs.

"The fact that I'm sitting here behind this desk in this magnificent church," Emanuel says, "is because of Jesse Norwood. He made us heroes in this community. What we did affected the whole community. Every week, people would go to church," he says emphatically, slapping his desk, "and then go to the Mohawk game. And now here I am, in a church of my own, serving the community. That's what Jesse Norwood was talking about."

The day Willie "Shoe" Lomax learned that lesson, about serving the community, serving a larger purpose, was a day he had some of the best stuff he would have at any time of his career. He remembers it well. He was unhittable that day.

He stood on the mound at Mohawk Park, their paradise, in the sunshine of a fall afternoon, rolling the baseball around in his left hand, his left arm draped behind his back, staring in at the plate. His pitching arm was warm and alive, crackling with energy. He'd only begun, but he'd already thrown nine strikes, nine untouchable strikes, sliders and curves, breaking in and away, enough to strike out a side, except he wasn't pitching in a game. He was pitching to Amos Otis. Big-league scouts for the Boston Red Sox, the last major league team to integrate, had brought Otis to Trinity Gardens to work out against the Mohawks in order to gauge his talent. Amos wasn't looking so good at the moment. Shoe had him looking like a child up there.

As a schoolboy, Otis had broken all the scholastic hitting records in Mobile County. During the summers of those years, playing for the Maysville team in the junior sandlot league, Otis was known for "messing up" otherwise excellent performances turned in by some of the Prichard Apaches best pitchers, James "Popcorn" Campbell, for one. The Apaches were, in effect, the farm team for the Mohawks, another development that Jesse Norwood adopted from the big-league model, Branch Rickey's model, where the next wave of little bitty babies was groomed, literally—"Yes, sir," Madison says, "we gave those boys haircuts, we made sure they had shoes, we took care of them. Isn't that right, Lyonel?" Pugh nods his head, but doesn't say anything—and coached in baseball fundamentals. After the Mohawks had built their field in Trinity Gardens, Jesse kept the lease on the land at Dozier's Alley. That's where the Apaches played. And after his return from Virginia, Pugh started coaching the new team, all those young boys who now dreamed of becoming a Prichard Mohawk, of wearing one of those jackets. Amos Otis liked to wreck those dreams.

"Amos did good, real good," Pugh says, remembering. "He sure liked to mess up Popcorn's games."

Campbell stands in the back, remembering too. He wasn't fully developed during those times as the pitcher he would become, and probably wished he could have been on the mound the day Otis was trying to show the big league scouts how he could hit. By then, Jesse Norwood, who all but single-handedly raised him, was calling young Campbell "the man with the golden arm." He had a powerful, frightening right arm. But Mr. Jesse had chosen Lomax, more seasoned and left-handed, to pitch to Otis to give Amos the best chance to shine in front of the scouts.

Then Lomax started breaking off that ungodly stuff. He'd taken Otis through most of his repertoire, starting him off with his roach ball, a nasty slider that disappeared as it broke over the plate.

Shoe didn't name the pitch the roach, he says. He wouldn't do that. Other guys on the team, the talkers like Candyman, or Willie "Sleepy" Burns, who taught Lomax much of what he knew about pitching, they liked to name pitches, said *everyone* named their pitches, just like Satch.

After Otis missed that one by about a foot, Shoe gave him the deuce, his Monroe curveball, named after the roller coaster out at Monroe Park, which Shoe had never even seen. And then the kidney bean, his forkball.

When he was learning the pitch, Shoe had asked Burns, "Why they call it a forkball, Mr. Sleepy?"

"'Cause it breaks into hitters, bites into their wheelhouse, and they damn near hurt themselves trying to swing with their hands all up under their ribs," Sleepy showed him, swinging with his hands tucked against his chest.

The ball felt so good in his hand. Shoe could read with his fingertips the red stitching and the scuffed hide, could hear unmistakably the ball's friendly intention to serve him, as he rolled it around, contemplating his next offering. And he could tell that those scouts beyond the backstop fence were looking at him now, with their notepads and stopwatches. He knew when he was being watched; he'd been there before.

From his position in deep center field, Emanuel recognized the grip Lomax had settled on, and he recognized the situation. He sprinted in toward the mound, calling, "Shoe! Shoe!" before Lomax could start his windup.

Mr. Jesse joined them on the mound. Emanuel said to his pitcher, "Shoe, they're trying to *sign* Amos. Give him something he can hit."

Lomax turned to look in at Otis, then glanced a little to the left of the plate to look at those scouts again.

Mr. Jesse told him, "Give Amos a chance."

Lomax understood, said, "All right." And then, he says, he "let up," and grooved a fastball that Otis could hit.

Amos smacked it down the left field line. And then he walloped another one, harder and farther, down the opposite baseline. Once he found his stroke, he was able to handle Shoe's breaking stuff, and it wasn't long before he was putting everything Shoe pitched into play, running the bases, leaving those scouts gawking at their stopwatches, signing his contract, and heading off for an all-star stint in the show.

In later years, after he had retired as one of the most popular Kansas City Royals—along with Frank White, Hal McRae, Freddie Patek, and of course, George Brett, who could have run for mayor—Otis became one of those Mobile-born players who would say there were others back in his hometown who were better than he was, his two brothers, especially. But if he ever forgets how many times he swung and missed against Lomax that day—as if ballplayers *ever* forget their numbers—Emanuel says he reminds him.

"Oh yeah," the captain says, back in the Trinity Gardens assembly hall, "whenever he's back for another award, or to attend some *gala* event, I tell him, 'Don't you be coming around here all uppity,'" he says, propping his hands on his hips and prissing a little. "'You wouldn't have made it but for me.'"

Emanuel laughs, laughs easily, as do the rest of them, without any trace of bitterness, though they have had to wonder from time to time over the years, what it must have been like for Amos and Cleon, and all those other ballplayers of whom they were the equals. They must have felt, during those moments of wondering, that they could have made it to the show as well, if only they'd been white.

Emanuel remembers being told as much when he was at Alabama State. "Oh yes," he says, "I remember *vividly*, playing exhibition games against white colleges. We'd beat the *pants* off those white boys, and those coaches would come up to me after the games saying, 'It's too bad *you're* not white.'"

"The Reverend Emanuel was *so* good," May adds, "Mr. Jesse would *pay* for him to come home on weekends during summer school just to play in our games."

Robert Emanuel Jr., sits behind Candyman in the aftermath of that praise with a gleam in his eyes, not overly proud. He *knows* he could play ball.

Willie "Shoe" Lomax knows the same thing, that he could play ball, and he'd heard the same thing, as Emanuel, as Satchel Paige, about the color of his skin. He was taken to Montevallo in 1963, in central Alabama, the midpoint in a triangle that had Birmingham, Montgomery, and Selma for vertices, all of them flashpoints in the civil rights struggle, where bombings and shootings, police dogs and water cannons were being employed to maintain white supremacy. He was brought there to work out with a San Francisco farm club, where he was told he could be the next Warren Spahn, the winningest left-hander in the history of baseball, the next Sandy Koufax—if only he weren't black.

Shoe's best chance to make it, everyone agrees, was in 1962. Early that year a scout for the Chicago White Sox, out of Birmingham, called him, said he wanted to sign him up. The plan was that the scout would come to Prichard the next time Shoe pitched, get some stats on him, and then come back the next time he pitched with some folks from the front office and the necessary paperwork. His next turn in the rotation came up against a team from Shreveport, Louisiana, a team they knew about.

"We'd played them before," Shoe says. "And we had a scouting report, something Mr. Jesse took care of"—something unheard of on the semipro circuit. "We knew their first six batters were killers. After them," he adds without a trace of irony, "it got easier."

Sleepy caught Shoe that day. Burns, a few years older than the others, had been with the team less than two seasons. While he grew up in the area, he'd been playing over in Mississippi, on the Moss Point team, which boasted a couple of other legendary Mobile natives, Delta Morris and Levi Washington.

They played in Mississippi for the money, the Moss Point team operating in residual versions of the old Negro Leagues, paid its players. Mr. Jesse took his young Mohawks over there as early as 1960. They remember that first encounter with those older, "professional" ballplayers *very* well.

"Those guys were *good*," May says.

"*Real* good," Madison adds.

Just as quickly, May says, "But we had 'em beat."

"Lyonel hit a home run that day, a three-run shot, wasn't it?"

"Yup," Pugh tells Sam. "Over the left field fence," he says, tracing the trajectory of that bomb in the air before him again, all these years later.

They remember that next door to the field was a busy nightclub, remember music playing during the game. Along about the sixth inning, they remember patrons drifting out of the club and walking over to the fence, some of the men holding bottles of beer in one hand, with their other arm draped across a woman's shoulders, coming to watch baseball, as word spread that some kids from Prichard were beating the mighty Moss Pointers, a team that had been to the National Colored Baseball Championships in Wichita, Kansas. They remember those fans as being altogether different from the ones in Hattiesburg. These fans were knowledgeable, appreciative, cheering both sides in the contest, cheering for the game.

Shoe was pitching that day, but couldn't hold his

lead, wasn't quite in possession of his full arsenal. Those players were too big, too strong. Bennie Harris remembers a shot off Sleepy's bat, screaming straight at him at second base on one short hop. It ate him up, hit him in the stomach. He says it hurt for a week, that there was a bruise for two.

The next thing they know, Sleepy shows up at Mohawk Park, wants to play for Jesse Norwood, he was so impressed with the team, with young Lomax. He gave up playing for money to come back to Prichard. Sleepy could play any position. He could have played on most any team he wanted to. He quickly became the elder statesman of the Mohawks, the one with the most experience and knowledge. He taught the younger players the intricacies and inside secrets of southern semipro baseball that only a player would know, which pitchers threw at you, the conditions of other fields—the infields with bad hops, the contour of baselines, outfield corners—the prejudices of certain umpires and fans alike. And he set about right away tutoring young Lomax on pitch selection and pitching strategy.

Sleepy didn't necessarily have to instruct those around him in order to teach. All they had to do was listen in to his nonstop chatter. Any position he played, he played well, and that's where the learning started. From his firstbase position he would take up after a runner, calling to everyone else, "Did you see how he hit the inside of the bag with his right foot?"

circling back around and repeating the maneuver once the runner had stopped and time was called. Sleepy was constant motion and constant dialogue, in practices *and* in games. He was anything *but* somnambulant—everyone says he got his nickname for other reasons. From deep in the hole at shortstop he would shift the rest of the infield based on the batter's stance in the box, saying, "Watch the front foot, where it's pointed, where it lands after practice swings." In the outfield he'd shift players based on the pitcher's grip on the ball, and from the bench he'd call pitches shortly after they left the pitcher's grasp from the rotation of the ball. All the Mohawks, most of the rest of them just as young as Lomax, had to do was listen to Sleepy.

From time to time, as Shoe tells it, Sleepy would interrupt his general discourse and give Lomax some specialized instruction. Able to see the pitching promise in the rough young boy's throwing motion, he taught him how to throw a breaking ball, a forkball, said that with a forkball and a standard hook "managers won't know *who* to send up to the plate."

Shoe was so raw at the time, he didn't even have his own spikes, had to borrow some from his uncle Albert. The shoes were not an exact fit, though, and every once in a while, if Lomax got really wound up— "a gen-u-ine whirling dervish," Candyman says—a shoe would come flying out, like debris from a twister. Sleepy would hustle in from whatever position he happened to be occupying, talking, "Now *that's* what I call follow-through. Did y'all see that?" retrieving the shoe. "Oh, Shoe, they won't know *what* to do about you!"

"Yes, sir, that's how it started," Willie says, of his nickname, sitting stately, regally, almost, in the middle of a couch in a reception room off of the main sanctuary of the New Light Baptist Church where he is the minister, the Reverend W. L. Lomax.

Under Sleepy's guidance, Shoe struck out four of those first six Shreveport hitters, pretty much all the numbers the Chicago scout needed, and went on to pitch a complete game victory, winning 3 to 2.

The scout said he'd be back in a week, with a White Sox general manager and a contract. But Shoe couldn't make the scheduled start.

"Oh, man," May says, cradling his head in his hands.

Shoe smiles. Some of the others, Pugh, Madison, snicker a little. Emanuel just sits there shaking his head. It's a few minutes before any of them will pick up the story.

"Man, oh, man," Ellis finally says. "That was all my fault."

"Aw, Sweet," Pugh tells him, "we all went along."

"We *had* to," Emanuel says.

It's not something Mr. Jesse ever knew about. At least he never let on that he knew of their late-night escapades. Occasionally, once they were old enough to drive, after the Saturday night meetings, the team hung out a little longer together, to talk baseball, to be together. One of their favorite spots was across Mobile Bay, a catfish house over in Spanish Fort, the Bay House.

"Far enough away so that Mr. Jesse might not hear about it," May confesses.

At the club, tucked away in the woods of the bluff that overlooked the causeway linking Mobile and Baldwin Counties, overlooking the Mobile delta where five separate river systems converged to feed Mobile Bay, they ate fried catfish, served up sizzling hot, the grease draining onto yesterday's newspaper, the meal completed with hush puppies and a mound of coleslaw. They drank beer, except for Emanuel and Lomax, and listened to blues singers accompanying themselves with a string guitar and a harmonica.

Shoe got a fish bone stuck in his gums. By morning the fever was so high he had to be hospitalized, had to miss the game, his chance to pitch in front of the Chicago brass.

Instead, the White Sox extended an invitation to Lomax to attend their training camp in Sarasota the following spring. When he got there, he was one of five black players. There were seventy-five to a hundred players who were white.

"But I'm not sure what happened," he says, shrugging. He remembers a Cleveland scout pulling him aside one day, praising his stuff, asking him to pitch to some slugger. He's not sure who. Might have been Killibrew. The scout had Shoe throw him some fastballs first, which were pounded out of the yard, then told him to go ahead and work in some of his breaking stuff, sliders and curves and forkballs, all of which went untouched, were untouchable.

"I *thought* they were looking at me," he says. But he never heard from that scout or the White Sox people again, and went home to Prichard. "But that's all right," he says with befuddling equanimity. "I wouldn't a wanted to miss our season of '63 anyway."

Cleon Jones, who would make his first appearance in a Mets uniform that summer, called Lomax on the telephone upon his return, offering encouragement, as he was sure Lomax would make it some day. Cleon had every reason to be so optimistic. He had seen big-league pitching, and he had seen Lomax pitch.

Reluctantly, for he is fiercely quiet, Lomax says, "I pitched against him once in high school"—late in his high school career, after he'd just started to work with Sleepy. Cleon was playing for rival Mobile County High. "The first time he comes to the plate, I says to myself, I'm going to strike Cleon out. I wanted to do it in three pitches, but it took four. I started him off with a curveball, when I knew he'd be looking for my heat. Then I showed him the kidney bean, which looks a little like a fastball at first. So he moves up and over the plate, looking for more breaking stuff and trying to reach it early. He hadn't even swung yet, but

I knew he was dangerous. We all knew of each other. So I finally show him my fastball, but up and in, backing him away from the plate. So he's ready now. He's seen everything. He's pounding and wagging his bat and snorting up there, so I rear back and throw him a pitch I don't think he knew I had, a change-up. He was way out in front of it and couldn't hold back. I struck him out, everyone on the Blount side cheering, 'Shoe! Shoe!'

"Yes, sir, I sure won that battle. He *did* hit a home run off me the next time up," he adds, slyly, laughing to himself. "But I sure won that battle."

And that seems enough, to have played the game, to have fought those battles and won his share. Willie "Shoe" Lomax remembers the battles, remembers the victories, and he remembers plenty of near misses. He remembers taking a no-hitter into the ninth inning against the Theodore Bobcats, and he remembers that trip to Montevallo where he was told he was already big-league material, except for the color of his skin. He knows his only real chance had come back in 1962, and he'd missed it. By the time he'd visited Montevallo, both Cleon Jones and Tommie Agee, born five days and less than a mile apart in Mobile, were already on their circuitous way to one day roaming the outfield of brand-new Shea Stadium for the amazing New York Mets. And Amos Otis, who would, in a few short years, share that outfield with those two former Mobilians, on one of the biggest stages to be found at the time, was already erasing all the batting records back in Mobile, his ticket just waiting to be punched. Shoe's chance had come, and it had gone.

In the privacy of his church, the gleaming vestibule, sanctuary, and sacristy quiet and deserted on a weekday evening, Shoe will softly admit, "I've had some flashbacks," referring to the curious workings of fate. "But it's just like Mr. Jesse told us," he says about opportunity: The door's going to swing open; it won't stay open. They had to be ready, ready to step through, ready to pull someone along with them. Shoe was ready, for the most part, except for a late-night catfish bone, "And timing," James Harris would say.

"Mr. Jesse tried everything he could," Shoe says. He even arranged for Lomax to go to Grambling University through his association with Eddie Robinson, lobbying the famous coach to "give this kid a chance." When Shoe showed up at the tryout, he was recognized as the best pitching prospect there. But there were no scholarship funds available, so he returned to Prichard, again. Grambling, of course, is where Casey Stengel and the Mets discovered Cleon Jones.

"And Shoe would have been signed too," Theodore Sellers says. He knows. He was on that same university team with Cleon and might have been signed himself, except for an injured knee.

"God had other ideas," Shoe says. "I done my job. God just had other ideas," he repeats, as easy as that.

He's thankful for his time as a Mohawk, for those lessons he learned about baseball, and life. He's thankful to have played a part in helping Amos Otis through that door, satisfied by Amos's recognition of his effort.

"When he comes home, he shakes my hand, hugs my neck, says he wouldn't have made it without me."

"Or me," Pugh says, the most aggressive thing he says all day. "I'm the one who was batting to Otis that day, when they were watching his defense," Lyonel testifies, *his* satisfaction showing, something Jesse Norwood would certainly take pride in, his boys had grown into such men.

"A different door opened for me," Shoe says finally. "And I thank Mr. Jesse for that."

Lomax sits in the middle of his couch, his large black hands, wrinkled more than calloused now, folded in his lap. He looks about him with minimal motion of his head, at the nice furniture, out the window to the neat grounds, and down toward his polished shoes, and says, "I'm thankful for this," meaning his church.

Shoe talks long into that evening, about baseball, and life, answering all questions put to him without any pain or regret registering on his face or in his voice. They are fond, satisfying memories, and not even the racially motivated rejection he suffered seemed to disturb him much. "I've had some flashbacks" is all he'd say. Otherwise, he is content. He has his church, his ministry, though he would still pick up a baseball, he says, given time to get back into shape. Talking about a possible benefit game with the university team in town, he says, "I believe I could beat them."

And I believe he could, sitting across the room from that gracious, gentle man. One last, obligatory question put to Shoe that night, Would he do it all over again, given what he knows now?

Willie "Shoe" Lomax takes another inventorying look around the shadowed room with a slight grin on his face. "If I could wind up here?" he asks before answering, generously considering a question that didn't require an answer. "Yes sir, I believe I would."

It's the same answer all those men give, and you have to wonder how: how they've escaped being more affected by the tragic overtones of their stories—of being cheated out of their dreams. Though maybe there's something in the nature of dreams, and dreaming, that allows for their acceptance of the events they're chronicling.

"For most men the business of shifting and reworking dreams comes late in life when there are older children upon whose unwilling shoulders the tired dreams may be deposited," Roger Kahn writes. "It is a harsh, jarring thing to have to shift dreams at thirty, and if there is ever a major novel written about baseball, I think it will have to come to grips with this theme."[62]

*

W. P. Kinsella, in his novel about baseball, *Shoeless Joe*, has his narrator ask "Moonlight" Graham about dreams and reality, his dream of breaking into the lineup of the 1905 New York Giants, that dream fluttering away after only one half inning of major league playing time, and no at bats. "It would have killed some men to get so close," he says.

"If I'd only got to be a doctor for five minutes, now *that* would have been a tragedy," Graham answers.[63]

When he is asked what he thinks might have become of his life if he hadn't played for Jesse Norwood and the Mohawks, Lomax says, "I might a been in jail, or prison, or on the street." He says that most of the crowd he hung around with in his pre-baseball days ended up that way. He says the police would pick him up from time to time to question him about some of those guys, and that his uncle Albert was worried about him, told him to find new friends. But it wasn't until Jesse Norwood came to his house, talked to his mother about young Willie's life, and asked her to let him come to the ball field and play for the Mohawks that Willie started to turn that life around, and first learned *how* to dream.

Ed Charles, who grew up in Daytona Beach, saw Jackie Robinson there during his first spring training in the Dodgers organization, when Ed was twelve years old. He later played with Nat Peeples, and his career highlight was making the 1969 Miracle Mets team, joining Cleon Jones, Tommie Agee, and Amos Otis. He says, "My dreams were limited. I couldn't dream the type of dream that a white could dream and really work toward realizing it." Then he adds, "It was against the law to work out these dreams. There were signs saying Colored Only here, Whites Only there. You could be put in jail or beaten up if you disobeyed."[64]

That is perhaps the greatest tragedy of all, that these men were born into a life so prescribed that even their dreams had limitations and they couldn't really know *how* to dream. But because Jesse Norwood showed Willie and all those other boys, that, yes, you *can* dream, that there is no law that can keep you from dreaming, they can say, honestly, forty, fifty years later, that they would do it all over again.

Shoe is living his dream. He says he has a doctorate of ministry now and spends time traveling as a guest speaker or a panel member, "Every once in a while," he says, in a cadence you suspect he picked up as a Mohawk, a cadence that lends itself quite naturally to the pulpit, "every *once* in a while, someone at those conferences from those days recognizes me and will call out, 'Shoe! Shoe!' Most of the time people call me Doctor, or Reverend, except every once in a while," he repeats, smiling broadly at the memory. "Other folks around me ask what that means, and I usually don't tell them." Shoe pauses, as if debating with himself, before adding, "But man, that brings me all the way back, brings it all back, and that sure is nice."

Six

*T*he sentiment that they would suffer the limitations and sacrifices all over again, without regret, is especially believable coming from Lomax and Emanuel. As ministers in their respective Baptist churches, they are latter-day examples of what DuBois called in his 1903 *Souls of Black Folk*, "the most unique personality developed by the Negro on American soil."

The Negro preacher, over the course of hundreds of years of slavery, became both the repository of any vestiges of African heritage and the leader of the way into fully Americanized life. He was the overall arbiter of all decisions allowed within the confines of plantation tribal living and the spokesman for the emancipated slave's introduction into the brave new world of so-called freedom. Descendant of the African high priest, these "medicine men" fulfilled roles of bard, physician, judge, and priest within the rapidly Christianized slave system and then within the earliest autonomous African-American institution, the Negro church.

In 1867, the year that found Henry Martyn Robert contemplating America's disorderly society out in San Francisco, the Reconstruction Acts were passed, redistricting Southern states and requiring their constitutions to address universal manhood suffrage in response to implementation of Jim Crow laws in the South, and the birth of the lawless Klan in Pulaski, Tennessee. In 1867 in Montgomery, Alabama, Nathan Ashby and some seven hundred Negro communicants marched out of the First Baptist Church to establish their own site of worship. The congregation declared its independence as the First Baptist Church (Colored), the first free Negro institution in Montgomery.

Baseball's color line was initially drawn in 1867 too. The game's first league, the National Association of Base Ball Players, a loose affiliation of more than two hundred amateur clubs, whose main function resided in policy and procedural governance, was the architect of that barrier, without which the entire history of the struggle for civil rights might have been different. At their annual convention in Philadelphia, the membership nominating committee was unanimously "against the admission of any club which may be composed of one or more colored persons,"[65] upholding the exclusion of the Philadelphia Pythians, "one of the most prominent Afro-American baseball clubs in the 1860s,"[66] from the state chapter of the association two months earlier. The reason given for the league's action was "to keep out of the convention the discussion of any subjects having a political bearing."[67]

The dilemma of what to do with the nation's four-and-a-half million new citizens, its freed slaves, certainly was such a subject. Arguments raged in the United States House of Representatives and the Senate about justice for the former slaves. And in the South, political maneuvering to maintain the bondage of black citizens, with Black Codes restricting their movements and rights, made a mockery of any notions of freedom or emancipation. "The Negro *was* a political subject in 1867," according to Robert Peterson, "but politics was a secondary consideration for the NABBP. Simple prejudice brought baseball's first color line. The members of the Association were all Northerners, but most shared with Southerners the belief that the Negro was inferior and not fit company for white gentlemen,"[68] in what was still considered a genteel, amateur's game, baseball. The Pythians, Michael E. Lomax writes, "exemplified the quest for self-determination among Afro-Americans in the post-Civil War era. Baseball became a vehicle to assimilate within the fabric of mainstream America and simultaneously elevate the status of Afro-Americans. Regardless of whether a black team won or lost, a championship between blacks and whites would serve to eliminate racial barriers and establish a sense of equality in the minds of blacks."[69]

The association wouldn't survive the game's looming professionalization, and with its passing, the color line would fade, some, but it would not disappear.

Its successor, the National Association of Professional Base Ball Players, formed in 1871, "never had a written rule against Negro players. It did not need one, for there existed a 'gentlemen's agreement' barring Negroes from this first professional league and from its successor, the National League."[70]

That did not mean that blacks weren't playing baseball, of course, only that they were overlooked by association clubs. Much as the celebrants had walked out of that Montgomery church to stake their own claim for worship, all-black teams were already sufficiently organized by 1867 to stage interracial challenge matches for baseball supremacy.

The popularity of baseball in these years and the explosive growth of Baptist membership rolls may be linked to the Civil War. In the aftermath of that horror, where hundreds of thousands of Americans died for the ideals of equality and union, Lincoln's war for sacred justice, equality of any kind was still just a dream, would remain a dream for another hundred years, except on the ball field, when it was allowed, and before the eyes of God, in church. The freedom to worship however one might, and the freedom inherent in any sport, but especially baseball, eclipsed politics and bigotry, if only briefly, in part, because of the participatory aspects of both. The raucous call and response of the Baptist church service can be likened to a true communion with God, a direct dialogue. And as for baseball: "Being a serious baseball fan," George Will writes, "meaning an informed and attentive and observant fan, is more like carving than whittling. It is doing something that makes demands on the mind of the doer. Is there any other sport in which the fans say they 'take in' a game? As in, 'Let's take in a game tomorrow night.' I think not. That is a baseball locution because there is a lot to ingest and there is time—although by no means too much time—to take it in."[71]

Albert Spalding, an early participant, governor, and innovator of the game, equated the growth of the sport with the fans' increasingly sophisticated ingestion of the sport. "It must be admitted that as the game of Base Ball had become more generally known; that is, as patrons of the sport are coming to be more familiar with its rules and its requirements, their enjoyment has immeasurably increased; because, just in so far as those in attendance understand the features presented in every play, so far are they able to become participators in the game itself. And beyond doubt it is to this growing knowledge on the part of the general public with the pastime that its popularity is due [where] all America has come to regard Base Ball as its very own, to be known throughout the civilized world as the great American National Game."[72]

Decades before Spalding's spurious claim that baseball was America's "very own" game, it was the de facto national pastime, though later writers, Koppett, for one, trace its derivation from imported lawn games such as cricket and rounders. Spalding can be forgiven his myth-making, as he was far from alone in his fervor. Far from the story that the quaint exercise was "invented" by Civil War Major General Abner Doubleday and disseminated by discharged soldiers after Appomattox, the game was already widely popular in the North, and the rural South, a plantation sport played by both planters and slaves. Clarence Darrow said of his Ohio boyhood in the 1860s, "I have snatched my share of joys from the grudging hand of Fate as I have jogged along, but never has life held for me anything quite so entrancing as baseball."[73]

Mark Twain declared baseball, "the very symbol, the outward and visible expression of the drive, and push, and rush and struggle of the raging, tearing, booming nineteenth century!"[74]

Walt Whitman, poet, Lincoln eulogist, admired baseball's "snap, go, fling of the American atmosphere—[it] belongs as much to our institutions, fits into them as significantly as our constitutions, laws: is just as important in the sum total of our historic life."[75]

In reality, though, some of those who controlled the game in its early years blatantly flouted tenets of the constitution. An 1868 want ad in the *Brooklyn Eagle* reads: "The National Club of Washington are looking for a first baseman about here." But, "No Irish need apply."[76]

It was common practice for some teams to selectively exclude other fractions of American society, most notably Jews and blacks, though any roster of the game's earliest icons, Matthewson, Cobb, Wagner, and McGraw, attests to the limited nature of such parochialism.

The names of celebrated Negro players infiltrated the lineups during those initial years of professional baseball too. Bud Fowler is recognized as the first black professional player—he broke in as the second baseman for the New Castle, Pennsylvania, team in the early 1870s. Fowler spent his boyhood in Cooperstown, New York, in fact, where Spalding's faulty legend has the first baseball game played in 1839. Moses Fleetwood Walker became the first black major leaguer when he played for Toledo of the American Association in 1884, the year Leonard Koppett records as that of the game's first true World Series, between Providence of the National League and the association's New York Metropolitans. Likewise, a Negro championship of Georgia was played as early as 1884, between teams from Atlanta and Savannah. Walker was born in Mount Pleasant, Ohio, in 1857, which at the time was a way station on the Underground Railroad. His father was a businessman in town. In 1877 Walker was in Oberlin, Ohio, taking preparatory courses for Oberlin College. Oberlin was a hotbed of abolitionist sentiment before and during the war and also a stop on the Underground Railroad.

All of that early training, and his bitter baseball experiences (he retired from the game in 1890 after being dropped by Syracuse's International League team) would prompt him to write, in 1908, *Our Home Colony—A Treatise on the Past, Present and Future of the Negro Race in America.* In the pamphlet he characterizes the years after emancipation as the "colonial period" in the American Negro's development, where "American people were in no way prepared to accept the Negro with full equality of civil and political rights."[77]

Although lettering every year at white, liberal Oberlin, and two additional years at the University of Michigan, Walker's first season with Toledo created racial problems. Cap Anson, then manager of the Chicago White Stockings and one of the most popular and influential players of the era, threatened to boycott an exhibition game in Toledo if Walker played. Walker, a precursor to more militant African-Americans like DuBois, Marcus Garvey, Malcolm X. and James Baldwin, advocated in his frustrated post-baseball years a blanket emigration of black Americans to Africa. He was the first, before Garvey, to call for the establishment of a New Liberia. He went so far as to proclaim that émigrés should be forced to leave, because there was "nothing but failure and disappointment" for the American Negro.[78]

In 1886, twenty-one-year-old Frank Grant entered professional baseball as an infielder for Meriden,

Connecticut, an Eastern League team. Grant "was probably the best of the black players who appeared in white leagues during the early years. He was a strong hitter, and his play at second base earned him the sobriquet 'the Black Dunlap,' a signal compliment, because Fred Dunlap, the St. Louis second baseman and the first player to reach the $10,000-a-year salary level, was regarded as the best at the position."[79] Grant is credited with the advent of the feet-first slide in baseball, not as its practitioner but as its target. In 1890, Ed Williamson, former big-league shortstop, writing for *Sporting Life*, says Grant was the first infielder to wear shinguards, because "haughty Caucasians" of the International League had taken to utilizing the new slide into second base in lieu of the traditional head-first dive, making "it their special business in life to spike [the] brunette Buffalo,"[80] Grant.

With those three, along with George W. Stovey, the first great Negro pitcher, making headlines playing the white leagues by 1886, the season of 1887 brought about even greater promise for Negro players in organized baseball, with at least four others on the rosters that spring, possibly more. Sol White, whose *History of Colored Baseball*, published in 1907, provides an invaluable record of those early years, entered organized baseball in 1887, on the Wheeling club of the Ohio State League. Fleet Walker's younger brother, Weldy, who would become the second black major leaguer, played in the same league that year. In *Only the Ball Was White*, Peterson adds, "Exciting the fancy that more Negro players would gradually be absorbed into organized baseball's structure was recognition of the new League of Colored Base Ball Clubs as a legitimate minor league under the National Agreement."[81]

Despite the league's rather quick collapse, White saw reason to be optimistic, because "the short time of its existence served to bring out the fact that colored baseball players of ability were numerous."[82]

Grant batted .366, under the old rules but had 48 extra base hits and 40 stolen bases in 105 games; Fowler batted .350 and stole 30 bases in 30 games; Walker had 36 thefts in 69 games; Stovey won 33 games as a pitcher; and Bob Higgins, another pitcher in the International League had a record of 20 and 7. There was hope, what with all these players playing well, even brilliantly in some instances, for ever more black players in the "national game," rendering entrenched racial barriers based on inferiority unsupportable in society at large, and more important, in the minds of the country's black citizens, if not in actuality.

But the 1887 season also showed the irrational grip racism could claim on the soul of America, in the North, as well as the South. Surfacing that year in Syracuse, New York, of all places, were "the first serious rumblings of player discontent that spelled the beginning of the end for Negroes in the early white leagues."[83] Two Stars players refused to sit in on a team promotional photograph because Higgins would be included in the portrait. "Dug Crothers Suspended," the headline in the July 11 issue of *Sporting News* read, for "refusal to sit beside the colored pitcher."[84]

A month later, the league's directors held a meeting to hear players' grievances. *Sporting Life* reported: "Several representatives declared that many of the best players in the League were anxious to leave on account of the colored element, and the board finally directed Secretary White to approve no more contracts with colored men." So it was finally on paper. Peterson writes, "For the first time, a professional baseball league had drawn the color line officially."[85]

That same day the Newark *Evening News* published an announcement that Stovey of the Newark Little Giants would pitch in an exhibition game against the major league Chicago White Stockings and the great Cap Anson. Anson, true to his old biases, refused to field his team if Stovey took the field. The big left-hander's absence was attributed to sickness, though the real story was reported by *Sporting Life* a year later.

Two months later, the St. Louis Browns added their voices to the din, refusing to play an exhibition game against the all-Negro Cuban Giants. The Giants, who were definitely not Cuban, passed themselves off as having Caribbean roots simply because they wanted to be part of the baseball world. And they were good, having lost an exhibition game to the Detroit Wolverines (later to become the Tigers), 4 to 2, after leading in the eighth inning. *The Sporting News* wrote that the "Cubans" were "equal to any white players on the ballfield."[86]

The Wolverines, it should be noted, won the "world championship" that year, defeating the American Association's Browns in a fifteen-game series.

By 1888, reconstruction was a distantly remembered rumor. In its place were chain gangs, sharecropping peonage, Jim Crow transportation, miscegenation laws, and restrictive suffrage statutes. And now official inequality was steadily progressing on the baseball diamond. "If anywhere in the world social barriers are broken down it is on the ball field," the Newark *Call* declared in a scornful editorial after the International League convention of 1887. "There many men of low birth and poor breeding are the idols of the rich and cultured; the best man is he who plays best. Even men of churlish disposition and coarse hue are tolerated on the field"—referencing Anson perhaps, whose racial slurs could be characterized as churlish and coarse, at the very least, if not ironic, coming from the first white child born in Marshalltown, Iowa. "In view of these facts the objection to colored men is ridiculous,"[87] the *Call* continued, stating the obvious. (These developments came less than a year after the Statue of Liberty, the beacon of freedom, was dedicated in New York harbor.)

Attrition came fast for Negro ballplayers in any white league, and there were no such players from 1892 to 1894. The only all-black professional team in operation during that time was the Cuban Giants. In 1895, Booker T. Washington, delivered in an address at the Cotton States Exhibition, what would become known as the Atlanta Compromise, acquiescing to racial inequality, in accordance with a perceived national consensus. A year later, the Supreme Court, in *Plessy v. Ferguson*, would write Jim Crow segregation into national law. By 1898, the last door opened by the bloody war fought for union and equality had been closed. The era of cooperative play ended when the last Negro team of the rollicking early days of organized baseball, the Acme Giants, folded.

Black ballplayers would still play the game, for it is an indomitable game, but for the next fifty years those players would operate in the relatively obscure though fabled Negro Leagues, making a mockery—for anyone who witnessed those games or those players, the likes of Paige or Gibson, of Cool Papa Bell or Smokey Joe Williams—out of Spalding's or Whitman's or Twain's naïve claim that baseball embodied or represented America in any sense of the word.

What was left girdering the new, black population of America—in the South at least, where more than 90 percent of that population lived—was the Baptist

Church, and its Negro preachers, though even that development is not without its ironies. DuBois traces the development:

"By the middle of the eighteenth century the black slave had sunk, with hushed murmurs, to his place at the bottom of a new economic system, and was unconsciously ripe for a new philosophy of life. Nothing suited his condition then better than the doctrines of passive submission embodied in the newly learned Christianity. Slave masters early realized this, and cheerfully aided religious propaganda within certain bounds. The long system of repression and degradation of the Negro tended to emphasize the elements in his character which made him a valuable chattel: courtesy became humility, moral strength degenerated into submission and the exquisite native appreciation of the beautiful became an infinite capacity for dumb suffering. The Negro, losing the joy of this world, eagerly seized upon the offered conceptions of the next; the avenging Spirit of the Lord enjoining patience in this world, under sorrow and tribulation until the Great Day when he should lead His dark children home—this became his comforting dream."[88]

Such religious fatalism, he says, "painted so beautifully in *Uncle Tom*," leads to a sullen hopelessness replacing hopeful strife, leads, even, to Washington's Atlanta Compromise: "In all things that are purely social we can be as separate as the fingers, yet one as the hand in all things essential to mutual progress," Peterson writes.[89]

Separate, the promise claimed, but equal. And yet, without any economic or political leverage, without educational opportunities for more than industrial utility, equality was never fully realized in any arena, reducing DuBois's race of "dark children" to a life lived that was all but indentured. A veil separated the races whereby blacks operating within society could only see themselves through the eyes of whites. Their self-worth and self-knowledge were filtered through the expectations and assumptions of others. DuBois called instead for an educated elite, a "Talented Tenth," to lift up the race, because at the very least, Washington's compromise—implicitly surrendering "inalienable" rights for the pursuit of assimilation into the industrial workplace and economic independence through remedial training— would require a vanguard of well-educated teachers and fully equipped schools. DuBois really thought this vanguard should insist, before all else, on those rights (the vote, civic equality, and educational opportunity) that Washington was seemingly relinquishing in the spirit of cooperative, though unequal, co-existence. It was an argument that would rage long into the next century and in some ways is still debated, an argument that pitted many successive black leaders against each other, just as it had those earliest statesmen. Was the integration of major league baseball worth the decimation of the Negro Leagues? Was school desegregation worth the ruination of the exceptional black schools such as Fisk and Spelman and Washington Carver? Was King's integration or Malcolm's nationalism the best strategy for achieving equality?

In the midst of that fray, sometimes at the forefront of it, stood the Negro Baptist preacher. The ministry was the only white-collar trade open to Negroes during slavery, "when it was a crime in all the Southern states to teach Negroes to read or allow them to engage in any business requiring the slightest literacy," as Taylor Branch writes. So "all roads converged at the Negro church. It served not only as a place of worship but also as a bulletin board to a people who owned no organs of communication, a credit union to those without banks, and even a kind of people's court."[90]

While Bud Fowler was in the earliest stages of his baseball career, the first black professional baseball career, a second exodus occurred in Montgomery when a contingent of the First Baptist Church (Colored) broke ranks and established the Dexter Avenue Baptist Church, where Martin Luther King Jr. would rise to the pulpit three-quarters of a century later. With those two separate developments, on the heels of the compromise of 1877, the staging ground would be set for the civil rights battles to come and for Jackie

Robinson's private war dismantling the color line in baseball.

It is neither surprising nor coincidental, this correspondence between religion, civil rights, and baseball. Having relied on plantation medicine men as their spokesmen, leaders, and healers, newly freed slaves naturally flocked to the churches, their first truly independent institutions. And it is just as natural that the little bit of freedom tasted there, the freedom to worship, would stir a yearning for more freedom, for a promised land here on Earth—separate, or shared, didn't matter. Their first glimpse of that promised land, for the duration of the game at least, was the baseball field, Giamatti's paradise.

"Paradise is an ancient dream," Giamatti says, "a dream of ourselves as better than we are, back to what we were." For "all play aspires to the condition of paradise," by which he means "to achieve a state that our larger Greco-Roman, Judeo-Christian culture has always known was lost. Where it exists, we do not know, although we have always envisioned it as a garden, sometimes on a mountaintop, often on an island, but always as removed, an enclosed, green place"[91]—the baseball field. And the sport that is acted out there is a ceremony that "mimics the ritual quality of religious observances," and in that mimesis, "an experience akin to the religious is engaged in over and over,"[92] by both participant *and* spectator.

For the sport's participant, it is an experience of

the constant dialectic of restraint and release, the repeated interplay of energy and order, of improvisation and obligation, of strategy and tactic, all neatness denied and ambiguity affirmed by the incredible power of the random, by accident or luck, by vagaries of weather, by mental lapses or physical failure, by flaw in field or equipment, by laws of physics that operate on round or oblong objects in their own way, by error in all its lurking multiplicity. It is not news that there is a snake of error in our lives; the news occurs when, for a moment, we can kill it.[93]

For the spectator, when we watch the sport, "and internalize the deep fact that this is an activity that has no ultimate consequence, no later outcome, no real effect beyond itself, we invest it with tremendous significance because in this world of history and work and endless, tangled consequence, to have no 'real' consequence or sequel is such a rare event."[94]

And if we watch long enough, we'll witness something like one of Hank Aaron's screaming home runs or Jackie Robinson stealing home or Satchel Paige striking out the side. And when we see something that surpasses "whatever we have seen or heard of or could conceive of doing ourselves, then we have witnessed, full-fledged, fulfilled, what we anticipated and what all the repetition in the game strove for, a moment when we are all free of all constraint of all kinds, when pure energy and pure order create an instant of complete coherence. In that instant, pulled to our feet, we are pulled out of ourselves. We feel what we saw, become what we perceived."[95]

In those moments no one—neither athlete nor fan—is marginalized. Everyone is free.

Is there any wonder, then, that Emanuel reports, "*Every* Sunday," emphatically, "people went to church, and then to the Mohawk game."

What they found in both arenas was hope. Hope for deliverance into an afterlife in the Christian church—what DuBois decried as a "sullen hopelessness" was hope, nonetheless, in an otherwise dour world. At the baseball field, if hope is the final refusal to give up, they found hope renewed inning after inning, and often enough, hope fulfilled. Not in the final score but in the play: Embedded within the timelessness of baseball, just as it is in the promise of immortality for the faithful, is hope, where everything that is good, better, best, is before us.

And what was hoped for in both arenas was freedom: the abstract freedom of everlasting life void of earthbound struggles and the freedom of choice, to play. "Baseball," Giamatti writes, "best mirrors the *condition of freedom* for Americans that Americans ever guard and aspire to." He goes on: "Baseball is part of America's plot, part of America's mysterious, underlying design—the plot in which we all conspire and collude, the plot of the story of our national life. Our national plot is to be free enough to consent to an

order that will enhance and compound—as it con-
strains—our freedom."[96]

But it wasn't until baseball desegregated itself
with the signing of Jackie Robinson, "the first American institution ever to do so voluntarily (before an
executive order desegregated the U.S. Army, and
before the Supreme Court, the public schools, and
Congress passed the Civil Rights Act of 1964),"[97] that
America lived up to its promise of the Declaration of
Independence and the Emancipation Proclamation
and played by the rules of the constitution and the
American dream. Robinson was on that field because
of his skill. Merit would win out. That was baseball's
promise, the hope it provided.

Such was the hope that inspired Hank Aaron. And
it was the promise Jackie Robinson helped deliver that
sustained Aaron's endeavor to break Ruth's record, as
well as Martin Luther King's larger crusade for civil
rights, among countless others. This was the hope
Jesse Norwood instilled in these men when they were
"little bitty babies," along with the promise that
opportunity would come. This, at a time when, Jimmy
Knight understates, "It was not good to be poor and
black in urban Alabama," referring to the gangs and
such. "They were going nowhere," he adds flatly.

And they knew it. Just as they knew all the
inequities and strictures designed to keep them that
way. "We knew all about that stuff," Reverend
Emanuel says. "But there wasn't much we could do

about it, except play baseball."

The rest of them shrug off the topic as well, as if there's no point in addressing it.

"We just played ball," Pugh says.

But Candyman has that steely, dead-red look in his eye. The subject does need to be broached, he seems to be saying. That part of the story is worth telling, needs to be told.

While Jackie Robinson's breaking down of baseball's color line did, in fact, change the way black and white Americans thought about themselves and others, integration did not end racism. More than a decade after Robinson's debut, these men were maturing into baseball players who might have been mentioned today in the same breath as Warren Spahn or Sandy Koufax, Brooks Robinson or Mickey Mantle, except they never really got the chance, not a fair chance, anyway. Not because of athletic inadequacy, but because of systemic racism. Not one of them, though, has brought along any thoughts of reparation or compensation or even apology. No, they're here because of what they were able to accomplish in spite of the prevailing conditions, how they picked their own selves up out of that depravity and can sit there with dead-red confidence and conviction. That's the story they want to tell.

"'Be a man,' Jesse Norwood taught us," Ellis May says. "No matter what you do."

The Reverend Emanuel offers an example: "I may

eat your free lunch," he says, "but not before I work for it."

Martin Luther King Jr., in his first published essay in April of 1956, put it this way: "We Negroes have replaced self-pity with self-respect and self-depreca-tion with dignity. In Montgomery we walk in a new way. We hold our heads in a new way."[98]

This came some six months into the Montgomery bus boycott, with hundreds of impoverished laborers walking to and from their jobs rather than submit to the city's bus laws. They had walked through the winter, and they would walk another six months before achieving success, but for King, success was already assured, through that newfound self-respect and dig-nity. King believed "that renewing, reforming, indeed revolutionizing individuals would reform and revolu-tionize society, more than the other way around."[99]

Part of King's conviction stemmed from a crisis in confidence earlier in that struggle. In the middle of a cold January night only a couple of months into the fight—after he'd received one of his first telephoned death threats, and three days before a bomb targeting his wife and baby girl blew up the front room of his parsonage—he prayed to God for the strength to con-tinue. He later told a lieutenant, Wyatt Tee Walker, that he took Jackie Robinson as his inspiration. "'Jackie Robinson made it possible for me in the first place,' King told Walker. 'Without him, I would never have been able to do what I did.'"[100]

To the assembled mob armed for revenge after the bombing, King said, "'God is with us. With love in our hearts, with faith and with God in front we cannot lose,'"[101] turning a certain bloody riot into a chorus of "Amazing Grace." It is altogether fitting, inspirational, even, that King's calming words, delivered before the backdrop of his bombed house, provoked the singing of that particular song out of the teeming desire for retaliation, a song penned by a repentant slave ship captain a century earlier. Correta Scott King picks out that moment, her husband's rallying conviction and the crowd's spontaneous response, as the defining moment of the civil rights movement. The model for such forbearance was Jackie Robinson, using the blueprint found in *The Life of Christ*, the correspondence of religion, civil rights, and baseball.

Recreation—the playing of a game, or sport; taking up a position on the baseball field—can be refigured as re-creation, "the making again according to some standard in the mind, vision in the head, in the hopes of making what one imagines palpable," something that begins as a "gnawing hunger" to somehow express how it *should* be, and then a "rage to get it right,"[102] if not perfect. Despite any outward pacifist countenance both men turned to the world at those moments of their respective, personal Golgothas, a seething hunger-turned-rage determined the paths of Jackie Robinson and Martin Luther King Jr. well before they set foot on those career paths, as a result of similar events, curiously, separated by only a few months, aboard buses, in 1944. Coincidentally, 1944 saw the publication of Gunnar Myrdal's *The American Dilemma*. It has been called the most influential book written about race relations in America and was cited in the *Brown v. Board of Education* decision. The dilemma Myrdal found was the contradiction between the ideals of individual liberty, equality, freedom, and justice so painstakingly spelled out in the American Creed—the Constitution, the Bill of Rights, and the Declaration of Independence—and the stark reality of life for the American Negro. This was the thing to get right.

"Three months before the Normandy invasion turned the tide against the Nazis, a fifteen-year-old black boy in Atlanta won a high school debate contest sponsored by black Elks. His speech was titled 'The Negro and the Constitution.'"[103]

Today 13 million black sons and daughters of our forefathers continue the fight for the translation of the thirteenth, fourteenth, and fifteenth amendments from writing on the printed page to actuality. We may conquer Southern armies by the sword, but it is another thing to conquer Southern hate.[104]

After delivering his winning oration, Martin

Luther King Jr. boarded a bus for the return trip from Dublin to Atlanta, Georgia. Along the route, he and his faculty chaperone were ordered by the driver to give up their seats for embarking white passengers. "'We didn't move quickly enough to suit him,' King recalled, 'so he began cursing us, calling us "black sons of bitches." I intended to stay right in that seat, but Mrs. Bradley finally urged me up, saying we had to obey the law. And so we stood up in the aisle for the ninety miles to Atlanta. That night will never leave my memory. It was the angriest I have ever been in my life.'"[105]

On the evening of July 6, 1944, one month after D-day, Lieutenant Jackie Robinson boarded a Southwestern Bus Company shuttle at Fort Hood, Texas. He saw a colored girl sitting in the middle of the bus and sat down next to her. Moments later the driver "stopped his vehicle and ordered Robinson to move to the back of the bus. As surely as Rosa Parks, but with no movement waiting to back him up, he refused to budge. The driver insisted. Robinson stayed put. White passengers became offended, particularly when Robinson, far from sitting silently, let the bus driver and anyone else who chimed in know what they could do with their ruffled feelings."[106]

The episode led directly to Robinson's discharge from the army later that year and, Falkner says, threw his whole future into doubt.

Worse things could have easily happened. In between the two incidents a black GI was killed by a bus driver in North Carolina. At a military base in Alabama, Joe Louis "was jostled by MPs after using a telephone in a white area of a bus station to call a cab."[107]

*

But coming to the army from UCLA, where he was a star on the school's integrated athletic teams— the first four-letter athlete in UCLA history— Robinson may have been less tolerant of the racial abuse he encountered throughout his short military career. His transfer to Fort Hood, a "hellhole" for black soldiers, resulted from a telephone tirade launched against a racist senior officer. Commissioned as second lieutenant in January of 1943, Robinson was the morale officer for a unit of black soldiers at Fort Riley, Kansas. Morale for any black unit was concerned almost exclusively with relations with its white counterparts. Jackie had called the base's provost marshal to complain about the seating arrangements at the installation's canteen, where black soldiers stood in long lines waiting for one of the few seats allotted to them while white soldiers came and went with ease.

"The major, who apparently did not know Robinson and who was lulled by his uninflected speech into thinking he was a fellow white, confided, 'Well, let's be reasonable, Lieutenant Robinson. Let me put it this way: how would you like to have your wife

sitting next to a nigger?'
"Robinson exploded."[108]

Earlier that year, Robinson wandered over to the baseball field after learning there was a notable squad of players in the camp, which included future team-mates Dixie Walker and Pete Reiser. But he was told he couldn't play, that he would have to play with the colored team, which was, of course, a cruel joke, since there was no colored team.

The following spring, at Fort Hood, after Robinson became a platoon leader for a company in the 761st Tank Battalion, Jackie rectified that recreational dis-parity, organizing his own team out of the men in his command. Much like the Tuskeegee Airmen, the 761st, an all-black battalion nicknamed the Black Panthers, "owed its existence and, ironically, its distinguished service record to the scorching insults of segregation."[109]

Originally based at Camp Claiborne in Louisiana, the battalion routinely encountered the embittering ills of segregation and racism both on base and, most especially, off base in Alexandria, where soldiers found themselves roughed up by local authorities and by patrolling MPs. Falkner describes an incident in early 1942:

"A black soldier was arrested and beaten by MPs in the Little Harlem area of town. The arrest provoked a confrontation that escalated to the point where groups of whites armed with pistols and shotguns confronted black crowds said to have gathered in the thousands. When word of this spread to Camp Claiborne, members of the 761st went into action: they took their tanks, loaded their guns, and rolled off toward the front gates of the base under the glare of spotlights and the booming of voices over loudspeakers. Only a hastily improvised negotiation prevented a full-scale assault on white Alexandria."[110]

In just another reaffirmation of the military's indifference to race relations, the battalion, a unit that would fight with distinguished valor in the heaviest tank engagement of the war under General Patton, was moved to Fort Hood within the year. Its living conditions at the remote and sequestered base were even worse, a squalid tent city reminiscent of something out of *Grapes of Wrath*, the leftover tents dating from World War I.

When Jackie hooked up with the unit and put together the baseball team, the men chipped in their own money, whatever money they could. "We put together patchwork uniforms, spent every cent we had on equipment—bats and balls. A single baseball got so incredibly beaten up, and yet they were precious to us. We held on to them for dear life," one of the players said.[111]

The balls were as precious as those Coca-Cola caps

would be to those boys on Bullshead Avenue in Prichard, Alabama, a decade later, a decade in which Myrdal had invested with the optimism that was at the heart of his analysis. Postwar America, he felt, after a history of its Creed and its "Negro problem" existing in agitated polarity, was in a position, globally (its Creed validated by the war) and economically to end the contradiction and resolve the "dilemma." But America did not. Not then, not soon enough, not quick enough. In some ways it still hasn't.

"It's a funny thing," Melvin Norwood said, of all the baseball talent rising from the mean streets of Mobile, where, according to Jimmy Knight, a nickel or dime was very hard to come by, for that bottle of Coke, its cap. "A funny, funny thing."

The "funny thing" is not that there was so much talent around. No, it's the harsh particulars of the time; for instance, had there been more baseballs, there would have been that much more baseball.

That there weren't more baseballs was evidence enough that America would not seize the chance to resolve its great dilemma. Municipally equipped recreational facilities would not sprout from the fertile territory of Mobile's black neighborhoods for decades, not before the city's political governance was revolutionized. From their foundational perspective, years before their voting rights as citizens of this country were guaranteed and enforced, the Mohawks had to be personally enfranchised in the endeavor. They had to, as King came to believe a couple of years later, reform themselves and those around them in order to revolutionize society. That is precisely the task that Jesse Norwood set before them, and exactly the contribution Branch Rickey through Jackie Robinson gave to baseball, sport, and America.

If Jackie Robinson revolutionized the way blacks and whites in America thought about themselves and others, that revolution sometimes had to occur at the most basic level of comprehension. One day very early on in that experiment, Rickey was sitting with Jackie's first skipper in the Dodgers organization, watching an intra-squad game during spring training. Jackie made a brilliant play at second base, diving for the ball, getting it back to his shortstop for a forced out. "Rickey thundered something about their having just seen a superhuman play.

"'Mr. Rickey,' [Clay] Hopper reportedly replied, 'do you really think a nigger's a human being?'"[112]

Rickey said nothing. He knew that Hopper's Southern upbringing had fostered that attitude. He knew that his beliefs were sincere. But the silent message Rickey and Robinson had for the rest of the world was this: "People, no matter their background, were basically fair; American democracy, even in the South, perhaps especially there, would always respond with willingness to give others a chance; and performance, in the end, mattered more than prejudice."[113]

It maybe sounds like the same kind of idealized optimism as Myrtal's, but at an individual level, it was an optimistically achievable goal, as Jackie Robinson soon showed. By the middle of the next season, his first on the Dodgers, Jackie, in winning over fans, teammates, and opponents, showed that America, the ideal expressed within its Creed, the revolution expressed in King's strategy, worked. The strength of Rickey's convictions—regardless of however much it was motivated by profit—and the courage of Robinson to enact them, proved America worked.

Or *could* work, so long as a Branch Rickey or a Jackie Robinson or a Martin Luther King Jr. was around to stand before history as a revolutionizing force. There would continue to be resistance and probably always will be. This is regrettable but it is nonetheless instructive to have to continually refigure, reaffirm, or reapply ideals. Not every individual, not the Clay Hoppers, Cap Ansons, and Dixie Walkers of the world, can be revolutionized.

The end of Jackie Robinson's baseball career, unfortunately, was tainted by entrenched racial overtones. With Rickey gone after the 1950 season, and O'Malley purging every vestige of Rickey's stewardship that he could, friction between O'Malley and Robinson—whom O'Malley intemperately called Rickey's prima donna—was inevitable. But Jackie thought it went deeper than that. "I knew what

O'Malley's problem was. To put it bluntly, I was one of those 'uppity niggers' in O'Malley's book."[114]

Finally, on December 13, 1956, O'Malley ousted Jackie Robinson, trading him to the New York Giants. "In the past," Falkner allows, "owners had been known for a certain clinical detachment in dealing popular but declining players"—as witnessed the Giants' own unceremonious dumping of Bobby Thomson a few years earlier—"but this seemed exceptionally mean [in its] unsparing lack of sentiment."[115]

Rather than submitting to the trade, choosing instead to capitalize on two lucrative offers beyond baseball—the vice presidency of Chock full o' Nuts and selling his exclusive retirement story to *Look* magazine—Jackie quit baseball. "The way I figured it," he has said, "I was even with baseball and baseball with me. The game had done much for me, and I had done much for it."[116]

Over the course of ten seasons, major league baseball had reformed itself to a point where black stars— Hank Aaron, Frank Robinson, Ernie Banks, and Willie Mays, among others—were numerous. But the game was still infected with old racial attitudes. And beyond the game, Jackie's retirement occurred a week before enforcement of the Supreme Court's *Browder* decision outlawing Montgomery's bus laws.

Earlier that December of 1956, King and the

Montgomery Improvement Association were busy putting together preparations for the centerpiece of the yearlong struggle, in anticipation of the edict. "In early December, commemorating the movement's first birthday, King opened the MIA's weeklong Institute on Nonviolence and Social Change with an address before several thousand townspeople and visitors at Holt Street Baptist Church.

"'God decided to use Montgomery as a proving ground,' he declared to the assembly, 'for the struggle and triumph of freedom and justice in America. It is one of the ironies of our day that Montgomery, the Cradle of the Confederacy, is being transformed into Montgomery, the cradle of freedom and justice.'"[117]

That wouldn't have been possible before Jackie Robinson. His "person and achievement was incontestable proof that such change was possible. His fame, and the inspiration he provided, was based on his dramatic and successful single combat against an institution that was a symbol of American culture. How much more could be done when a whole people rose up?"[118]

The goal of the institute was to train boycott participants for reconciliation with a hostile white majority. The boycott had been conducted in accordance with Gandhian nonviolent principles, and this new stage had the successful example of Jackie Robinson to draw on.

"If they call you names," the bus riders were taught, "do not answer. And if they strike you, do not retaliate." Love your enemies was the message. Embrace them. Win over their hearts, so that their attitudes might change.

At the same time, five days before his retirement, in accepting the NAACP's Springarn medal, Jackie Robinson spoke of the importance principle had played in his success. "It was principle, he said, that enabled him to endure those first years when the urge to quit was strong. It was principle that made him speak out rather than keep quiet."[119] The specific principles he was referring to were human dignity, brotherhood, and fair play, but he especially championed the blossoming struggle for human rights in the country, the Montgomery bus boycott.

There at the end of his baseball days, after ten years of shouldering the hopes of an entire race, placing himself as the bridge from hopelessness to opportunity—more of a burden than any single man should have to carry, one that doubtlessly shortened his life—Jackie Robinson turned his attention to Montgomery, Alabama, and the next man to take up the mantle of their race, Martin Luther King Jr., who already seemed destined for certain martyrdom.

Both men struggled with urges to quit early in their marches. After signing his contract with Branch Rickey in 1945, Jackie barnstormed with an integrated team that winter in Venezuela. His roommate on those junkets was Greg Benson, someone who was supposed to school Jackie in big-league pitching, big-league strategies. "Why did they pick me?" he reports Robinson asking repeatedly, unsure of his ability, or his resolve. There were, admittedly, better black ball players around, and more famous athletes.

King, chosen to lead the newly formed Montgomery Improvement Association even though he'd only been at Dexter Avenue and *in* Montgomery a little over a year, nearly bailed out just ten weeks into the Montgomery struggle, questioning his moral strength and his faith. Ralph Abernathy, in the pulpit of the First Baptist Church, had been there far longer. A decade before Jackie Robinson's entrance into Major League Baseball, Jesse Owens had humbled the Nazis and *their* notion of a superior race. Jackie's own brother Mack, an athlete Jackie admired and idolized, *should* have beaten Owens in the 200, and but for another twist of fate would have been a member of the relay team that trounced the stacked German one. A year later, A. Philip Randolph finally won recognition for the first black labor union, the Brotherhood of Sleeping Car Porters, after a decade of work, and on the eve of war organized a march on Washington that succeeded in winning concessions from President Roosevelt on job discrimination.

"Timing," James Harris has said, answering a similar question from the opposite end of the spectrum: Why *not* me?

Robert Emanuel sits there shaking his head. His

faith and his experience tell him the question is unan-
swerable, unnecessary, pointless, even. And yet it is,
Dr. King said, all about timing. "There comes a time,"
he preached to an assembly at Abernathy's First Baptist
Church, in the same moments when those bombers
were planning their assault on his residence, "when
time itself will bring about a change."[120]

"Accept your lot," Emanuel repeats, a lesson he
learned young, through the guidance of Mr. Jesse
Norwood, a lesson he teaches today. "Be the best
perch and accept your lot, even if it means these sacrifices," he says, gesturing about the room. Even if it
means sacrifice, the ultimate sacrifice of a Martin
Luther King, the relative sacrifice of Jackie Robinson,
or the minor sacrifice of James Harris. "If it's your lot to
be a street sweeper," the reverend had said back in the
offices of his church, "be the best street sweeper, the
Michelangelo, Beethoven, or Aaron of street sweepers."

When he says that, you wonder just how much
these men, as boys, knew of the world they found
themselves in, in 1950s south Alabama, how thoroughly they understood the constraints of that life.
And then you wonder how they can speak of it with
such poise and acceptance, the acceptance Baldwin
writes about on the centennial of Lincoln's Emancipation Proclamation. Could Emanuel have known, for
instance, that street sweeping was precisely the lot in
life Mack Robinson was relegated to upon his return

from Europe in 1936, after being hailed and feted across that continent in the aftermath of the Olympics as a conquering hero, dismissed and ignored back in his own country, unable to garner anything more than a nighttime street sweeper's job for the city of Pasadena? And could he have known that Robinson had been unable to accept that lot, would be fired from the job shortly thereafter? How did they sustain themselves? Where did they find any hope, or faith?

"Mr. Jesse Norwood," he says, evenly. Their faith was anchored by Norwood's promise that opportunity's door would open, they had but to ready themselves for that moment when "time itself would bring about a change," the epitome of hope.

"Genuine hope involves the recognition," Dr. King told his staff shortly before his assassination, "that what is hoped for is already here." He was paraphrasing counsel Christ had given his disciples, that they didn't have to wait for some distant day for the kingdom of God, it was already there, within them, "an inner power within you that drives you to fulfill the hope of a universal kingdom."[121]

Jesse Norwood's message was every bit the leap of faith those early persecuted Christians faced, yet he somehow imparted that message to those boys years earlier, along with the double-play, the hit-and-run, the sacrifice bunt. And they somehow learned it, used it to sustain themselves through those turbulent times of denial, disappointment, and sacrifice.

Jackie Robinson, fully aware of his brother's story, spoke of sacrifice, too, at the annual convention of the NAACP in Detroit in 1957. His closing address was on the need for sacrifice: "Everyone needed to give up something if the struggle was to succeed. Sacrifice was as old as history; sometimes it was grain, sometimes animals, sometimes even human life—but only by a willingness to surrender something of great value could results of great value be brought about."[122]

"That's right," Sam Madison says, and the rest of the Mohawk players nod along with him. There's reassurance in their eyes. Yes, it was unfair, inexplicably unfair. Yes, there had been sacrifices, small and large, sacrifices of time, or personal achievement, for others, for the team. But yes—and from the looks on their faces, there's no need to speak of the "great value" they derived from the experience—yes, they would do it again.

Then they turn to Jesse Norwood Jr., realizing, perhaps, that their sacrifices paled in the context of the discussion, that maybe they hadn't sacrificed *enough* to warrant the value returned. It's as if, recalling the man who orchestrated the endeavor, they considered the sacrifices he'd endured, and then the sacrifices of *his* son, who had to share his father with scores of other children and men, had to compete for his time. But Jesse nods along with them. He, too, wouldn't really have it any other way.

Seven

Jesse stops nodding and stares off into the back left corner of the room. An empty folding chair had been set out there in the shadows, one of the first things the Mohawks saw to upon entering the room. Occasionally throughout the gathering one or the other of them would turn and look over their shoulders in that direction. That is where their chief would have been sitting, where he always sat—apart from their business, overseeing, but leaving most of it to them, enfranchising them in this venture.

"You know," Jesse says, his hands in his pockets, head bowed a little. He favors his father. Jesse's taller than Norwood Sr., well over six foot, and solid. A former football player, he'd been courted by the Chicago Bears. A little lighter-skinned, he has the same round welcoming face as his father, the same smile. "I never really intended this to be all about my father," he says.

Ellis May has been fiddling with that Coke cap, flipping it over, spinning it on its edge. He silences that noise, trapping it under his right index finger, and says, "Your father gave us everything, Jesse. We had nothing."

In 1954 there was no city water in Prichard, Alabama. Many of the homes in the Mohawks' neighborhood still had outhouses. Only one household boasted a television set, a twenty-one-inch black-and-white Motorola that sold for the same price as a lot of land. There was no city transportation available. A baseball cost as much as a gallon of gas or a copy of *Sports Illustrated*, the very first issue of which was published in August of that year, with slugging Eddie Matthews of the Braves on the cover. The first color broadcasts of baseball televised the World Series in 1954, between the New York Giants and Cleveland. For the price of a color television set, you could have bought a whole block in Prichard. A newspaper, like a Coke, cost a nickel. For a dollar, they could have seen *On the Waterfront*, or *From Here to Eternity*, except there was no movie theater in Prichard. New to the bookshelves was *Fellowship of the Ring* and *Lord of the Flies*, stories of the quest to save Middle Earth and of the depravity of human nature.

"Nothing," Candyman says again, then picks up the Coke cap and tucks it safely back in his shirt pocket.

After a few moments Madison pipes up, "We had a mule!" and some of them smirk at the reference, until Jesse, shaking his head, an amused look on his face, says, "But *no* damn acres."

"No *sir*," Pugh answers. "No damn acres at all."

One mule, and one wagon they'd used to clear the lot off Victor Avenue in Dozier's Alley for their first ball field. Dozier was a real estate developer and home builder. He bought up abandoned shotgun houses and moved them to his "alley," then rented them out to itinerant pecan, potato, and cotton pickers. Jesse talked him into letting them use the low-lying parcel as a field, just as he had to negotiate with the city of Mobile to donate the dirt for their next field in Trinity Gardens.

"Mr. Jesse could negotiate with anyone," Pugh says. He would know. He spent some time in business with Jesse in later years.

"He commanded respect, from *everyone*," May says. "White *or* black." Jesse Norwood interceded with the local police whenever any of the neighborhood boys were picked up for infractions real or imagined. And he was one of the first community leaders contacted by Lowery, or Abernathy, or King for any kind of civil rights demonstration in the area. That's how much he was respected. "And he taught us that respect, for ourselves and others." Then May looks at the man's son and says, "This story *has* to be about your daddy."

"Mmm-hmm," the rest of them agree. "That's right."

"Well," Jesse Jr. concedes, "if ever there was a story of a self-made man, this is it"—self-made with less to draw on than these men had when they were boys back in 1954.

At the age at which they were playing corkball in the street, Jesse was pulling a coal wagon through the shantytown south of Ogelthorpe in Albany, Georgia, the center of the Velvet Corridor, where sharecropping, the bastard child of slavery, was the *best* hope for the state's extensive black population. "Coal," his voice echoed into the evening. Not yet a teenager, he already had the stout, compact body of a miner. His father dead, his mother gone to Mobile, Jesse had a little sister to support. When the Depression sucked the opportunity out of even that meager enterprise, and Eugene Talmadge was making life even more difficult for Georgia's blacks, he boarded a bus and brought Rose Marie to Mobile in search of their mother, and a job, while the world geared up for the Berlin Olympics, prelude to war.

Mobile, along with its port, boomed during the war years, its population swelling. Thousands of ships were built, and those ships moved more pulpwood than any other port in the world. Jesse found work down on the waterfront, just by showing up and being available, and eventually found himself aboard a Merchant Marine ship. Then he came home, settled in Prichard, in northeast Mobile County, started a family, and went to work at Brookley Air Station, about the time Jackie Robinson was being measured by Branch Rickey and the Dodgers, and baseball was becoming "the thing to do" in Mobile, was still the best hope for freedom for blacks anywhere in the South four-score and five years after Lincoln proclaimed them "thenceforward and forever free."

As when he was a child in Albany, Jesse, by the late forties, was bound by a life of necessity, with first-born son Melvin to support the year Jackie Robinson and the Dodgers came to Mobile, and namesake Jesse Jr. born the next year. And he was already starting to take an interest in the lives of young boys in the neighborhood. Willie Lomax remembers Jesse carrying him down to Mitchell Field or Prichard Park to watch young Hank Aaron, Billy Williams, and then Willie Burns, even older players like Lyonel Pugh's dad. There Jesse and the boys would retrieve one of the precious balls fouled out of the park and exchange them for admission to the game, the big man running along with the boys through the parked cars or into the woods after the cork-centered jewel patented by Albert Spalding.

No one knows the source for his love of the game, or why he never played it himself, but it's clear that his love was genuine, even infectious. Sister Rose, according to her son, Commissioner Sam Jones, was a notable corkball player herself, joining in on the street games, every bit the equal of some of the boys in speed and agility. He recalls her running and scrapping with the best of them, even disputing calls by the umpire, her big brother, Jesse. Sam is just one of the boys from the neighborhood for whom Jesse took on the role of father figure, especially after Rose passed at the young age of thirty-six in 1958. Sam moved in with Grandmother Lena after that, and Jesse would be there every Sunday morning for breakfast, a visit with his mother, with some lessons for young Sam, lessons in arithmetic, counting money, lessons on life, manhood. Sam spent his summers in the Norwood household, playing with his cousins, accompanying the family to the ball park on those Sunday afternoons, because, Jesse insisted, he needed to be around men.

Jackie Robinson, also fatherless at a young age, talks about the impact of surrogate figures during his turbulent, formative years in Pasadena. "I suppose I might have become a full-fledged juvenile delinquent if it had not been for the influence of two men who shared my mother's thinking." Carl Anderson, who worked in the mechanic's shop near where Jackie's Pepper Street gang hung out, took Jackie aside and counseled him against continuing with the gang activities, said that he was only hurting himself and his mother, that there was no future in following that crowd. "He said it didn't take guts to follow the crowd, that courage and intelligence lay in being willing to be different."[123]

The other man was a young minister, Reverend Karl Downs. When Downs arrived at the church that the Robinsons attended, he set out to connect with the church's youths, bringing dropouts back into the fold, even recruiting new families from the area. They staged dances for those young members, and Downs set up a badminton court on the grounds. "Many of the youngsters who began coming were finding the church an alternative to hanging out on street corners," Jackie says. "Karl Downs had the ability to communicate with you spiritually, and at the same time he was fun to be with. He participated with us in our sports. Most important, he knew how to listen."[124]

The thing that set the Mohawks apart, made them different, from the very beginning, was the organization. Too much of baseball in those years was anything but organized. Older players would congregate at parks around the area, choose up sides and stage a game. The littlest boys were relegated to the sidelines, watching those loose contests that were as much about drinking and gambling as about athletics. Between that unsavory exhibition and the idle youth who would gang together and gravitate toward trouble, Jesse Norwood first recognized a need for some other structure in the lives of these boys, and then an opportunity to provide that structure through his Mohawks.

"Jesse Norwood revolutionized sandlot baseball in Mobile," Jimmy Knight says. "The Mohawks had a manager, a general manager, uniforms, just like the pros," he says, counting off the relative novelties of Norwood's team on the fingers of his right hand while those Mohawks in the room nod in agreement. "Huge crowds would show up to watch," he continues.

"Huge," Madison says.

"He had rules, regulations, policies," Knight says. "If there had been three, four more Jesse Norwoods, there would have been sixty, seventy, a hundred more kids saved, kids who would have grown into productive citizens like these men," he says. "He started managers' meetings, drew up yearly schedules—these things were *unheard* of!"

But Sam Madison returns to an earlier point. "There were other men," he says. Sam's story, maybe because he spent so many years considering it a failure, compels him to insist that there were others. "They should all be heard." Others in the room do not disagree. "There was Pop Smith and Otis Nixon with the Prichard Athletics, James Robinson with the Plateau Bears, Pete Ryan out at Whistler, Ed Tucker down the street at Mitchell Field, and my first great coach, Mr. Hines, right here in Trinity Gardens."

The men all turn to acknowledge Mr. Hines, Earnest "Pop" Hines, who had managed the Blue Devils. A small man now frail in his eighties, Hines has been quiet throughout the discussion. He sits there with a satisfied look, shriveled right hand clasping the top of his walking cane, and utters the one thing he'll say all afternoon, "Jesse Norwood"—his contemporary, competitor, nemesis, and example—"was the greatest. We all looked up to him."

Sam first played for Hines when he was thirteen, in 1955, a year, a baseball season punctuated by Claudette Colvin, Emmett Till, and Rosa Parks. As a younger boy he played corkball with his brothers and other neighborhood youths. They couldn't even afford the nickel for a soda cap, he says. "We had to go around to stores asking for soda-water caps." Within a year or so, his friend Robert Emanuel started talking to him about coming to the Mohawks, telling him about the organization, the practices, the meetings. "'You might like it,' Emanuel said to me. 'Give it a try.'

"For two years he's telling me this. 'You might like it, Samuel.'"

Finally, Madison relented. He accompanied Emanuel to a team meeting, sitting off to the side, with Mr. Norwood.

"This was before the season started. They talked about baseball—who was going to pitch, the lineup for tomorrow's practice game. They talked about business, dues, and such. They talked about school, helping each other out with their reading, helping the younger boys with math. Reverend Emanuel was right. I liked what I saw.

"At the end Mr. Jesse turns to me and says, 'You play ball?'

"'Yes sir,' I said.

"'Then why don't you come out tomorrow and let's have a look.'

"That's all it took."

Sam went out to the Trinity Gardens park the next day and put on a display of batting, winning a spot in left field, displacing May yet again. And he got his Mohawks jacket.

"I felt so important when I put that jacket on."

He batted fourth or fifth in the lineup, he says, "for power, and pressure," unfolding two fingers of his left hand.

Mr. Jesse came to rely on Madison's big bat in crucial situations. "I need you, Bo," he'd say.

"Bo," Candyman repeats, as if just then remembering the nickname Mr. Jesse had given Sam.

"I need you to come through for me, Bo. I *need* you," he'd say.

"He taught us to have faith in ourselves," Sam says.

Emanuel looks over, says, "I *told* you."

"Yes, you did," Sam tells him, a big smile on his face.

"And Bo *always* came through," Pugh adds. "Tell him about that Monarchs game."

Sam's smile grows even larger, he says, "1967," but then stops, his smile fading.

"Go on, Sam," his friend Emanuel urges.

Then their president, Ellis May, says, "Tell it, Bo."

In 1967, the city championship tournament had come down to three teams, the Mt. Vernon Monarchs, the Prichard Athletics, and the Mohawks. The Monarchs were so good that year, they beat the Athletics to set up a winner-take-all contest on Labor Day. They played it in Prichard Park. Thousands of fans turned out. The game was so important that Mr. Jesse went to the medical center where Samuel Coates worked and talked his foreman into letting "Lank" off for the day.

"When Mr. Jesse came walking through that gate with Lank at his side, the crowd got *real* quiet," Sam remembers.

But Coates had an off day. And to make matters worse, Sleepy broke his thumb warming up Lomax. It was a tight game, Shoe and Mt. Vernon's Johnson swapping strikeouts. Both teams made superb plays on defense, the Mohawks, especially, with Pugh stabbing a line drive over the bag at third, Emanuel throwing out a runner at the plate, and Madison making a tough catch in foul territory.

Bottom of the eighth, the Mohawks are down, 2 to 1. Emanuel leads off with a double. Two ground outs later, he's on third. Ceding to conventional wisdom, the Monarchs decide to pitch to the cleanup hitter rather than putting the go-ahead run on base. Mr. Jesse takes that batter aside as he's choosing his bat, says to Sam "Bo" Madison, "I need you, baby."

Sam hit a home run over the short right field wall. The Mohawks went on to win the game, 3 to 2.

"Champions," May says, who by this time had gone into the service and come back, was no longer playing. He had taken his one at bat.

"You took one *pitch*," Pugh reminds him.

"Curveball," May admits. "I went back to the

bench and took off my uniform. That was it. I hate a curveball," he says.

The other players snicker. Ellis May had successfully dodged sniper's bullets in Southeast Asia, but couldn't stand in against a deuce back home.

Sam Jones was still in the service in 1967. Pugh was spending as much time on business as baseball. Lomax and Emanuel were looking forward to their ministries. Madison's family was growing. But Sam was the hero of the day, and the Mohawks were city champions again.

"After the game an Athletics scout came up to me and asked me how old I was," Sam continues. "When I told him I was twenty-five, he didn't say anything more, just walked away. I remember Yogi was standing beside me, and he said, 'You should have gone back in '61.'

"What do you say to that? I knew it was true."

"We *all* thought it was true," Emanuel tells him.

"But what do you say to that?"

The Mohawks don't answer, only dip their heads, lowering their eyes, letting Sam out of the spotlight.

"Greatest game of my life. I went over to the bench, sat down, started crying."

"What's the matter, Bo?" Mr. Jesse asked, finding him there.

"It had been building up inside of me for years, and I couldn't hold it down anymore."

"It's all right," Mr. Jesse said. "Tell me."

"I said to him, 'I failed you, Mr. Jesse.'

"He said, 'Naw, Bo. You didn't fail me. You've

never failed me. None of you boys have.' I just sat there bawling."

Ellis May, their spokesman in so many ways, asks Madison, "And what did he teach us about that?"

"That it's all right," Sam answers.

"It's all right," Candyman repeats.

The year of their first championship, the Gulf Coast Championship, was 1963, a year most of Alabama was embroiled in a white-hot struggle for civil rights, as were Georgia and Mississippi. And most of the rest of the nation was watching. Acting on King's earlier defiance of an injunction against protest marching, Birmingham sheriff "Bull" Connor jailed the civil rights leader just before Easter weekend, the traditional start of the baseball season. Connor had gotten his nickname, not for his Draconian efforts to stifle the protests nor for his stumpy physique, but from his days as a baseball radio announcer in the '20s. He was given to lathering over those broadcasts with otherwise inane chatter, "shooting the bull." Lionized by staunch white supremacists for his stance against equality, Connor proved to be merely a necessary pawn that needed to be manipulated for the success of the movement. In the end he was as ineffectual that spring of 1963—his own fire department ultimately refusing to turn on the water hoses, saying, "We're here put out fires, not people," while Connor shrieked, "Turn on the goddamn water!"—as he had been in a confrontation with Robinson ten years earlier. Jackie came to town that off-season of 1953, touring with a team of all-stars. Connor showed up at their hotel intent on enforcing a city ordinance against interracial athletic events. Not even bothering to interrupt his card game, Jackie sent word back to Connor through an emissary that the Bull could "kiss my black ass."

Jackie returned to Birmingham that spring of '63 to lend his support for King's struggle. To a boisterous, overflowing crowd gathered at Holt Street, he offered praise for their courage.

From jail King had issued a letter in response to a group of local clergy that had publicly criticized his actions as that of "outside agitator." He stressed the interrelatedness of *all* people. "Injustice anywhere is a threat to justice everywhere," he wrote. "We are caught in an inescapable network of mutuality, tied in a single garment of destiny. Whatever affects one directly, affects all indirectly."[125]

Another, louder and bolder, epistle was published that spring, James Baldwin's *The Fire Next Time*. In it, Baldwin—the same age as King, and like King, the son of a Baptist preacher, who had spent some of his formative years at the pulpit—urged his nephew, urged all blacks, to toughen up, build up their self-worth, and with religious guidance show compassion for each other *and* their oppressors. Racism, Baldwin believed at the time, stemmed more from ignorance than conscious intent. He warned, however, that those ways must change if we were all to avoid a racial Armageddon.

"If we," Baldwin wrote, "and now I mean the relatively conscious whites and relatively conscious blacks, who must, like lovers, insist on, or create, the consciousness of the others—do not falter in our duty now, we may be able, handful that we are, to end the racial nightmare, and achieve our country, and change the history of the world. If we do not now dare everything, the fulfillment of that prophecy, recreated from the Bible in song by a slave, is upon us: *God gave Noah the rainbow sign, No more water, the fire next time.*"[126]

It seems, though, that the apocalypse was already upon them. King's hotel was bombed some weeks later, as was his brother's house in Birmingham, prompting Robinson's visit.

In June, Alabama governor George Wallace barred the entry of black students into the University of Alabama, belligerently calling for "segregation forever!" Kennedy's federal marshals were called in to remove the obstruction. And that night the president gave the most impassioned speech he would give on the urgency for civil rights, asking Americans, "Are we to say to the world that this is the land of the free, except for the Negroes?" He then pledged his leadership to that cause, the "moral crisis" of the country, something King had been lobbying years for. But the next night an unseen assassin's bullet found Medgar Evers and he died in a pool of blood outside his home in Jackson, Mississippi. Just days before, he had told a reporter, "If I die, it will be in a good cause."[127]

In Georgia, the cause had been in motion for over a year, with nonviolent marchers seeking desegregation of downtown Albany being arrested if they dared to cross the east-west parallel through the center of town, Ogelthorpe Street. Student Nonviolent Coordinating Committee staff had been canvassing the area for support and registering voters.

In August, King led the mass march on Washington, where he delivered his "I have a dream" speech, rallying the nation behind a congressional initiative for civil rights. On the eve of that march, in his adopted country of Ghana, having succumbed to the hopelessness he predicted and witnessed and fought, W. E. B. DuBois died.

Only weeks after King had raised those hopes again, had given them wings with the power and poignancy of his sermon on the mount, the Sixteenth Street Baptist Church in Birmingham was bombed, killing four little black girls. Jackie Robinson, among others, could not accept what had happened and set out for Birmingham once again. He "went down there and walked over the rubble of the church," remembered Marian Logan, who accompanied him. "I can see him standing there with his fists shaking, trying to control his fury."[128]

That fury, the nation's fury, turned into shock two months later when Kennedy was assassinated.

In the midst of all this, Jesse Norwood guided and protected his former "little bitty babies," the now gentlemen Mohawks, ever vigilant about their moods and their actions. He neither denied nor ignored the events, even included some of the players in his work organizing nonviolent protests in Mobile. He lectured them against violent reaction, against hatred of any kind. And he held them to their task, baseball. He still believed that hope was the thing to be pursued, not vengeance. And he still felt that hope, and freedom, in the full light of all the bloodshed happening around them, was still best achieved on the baseball diamond.

And they responded in kind, maybe even channeling some of their anger into their game. Lomax won twenty-three games that year. Pugh, back with the team again, along with Madison, hit dozens of home runs. Emanuel stole bases at will. At a crucial juncture in the year, they played a home-and-home series against the Pensacola Seagulls. On their trip to Florida, the Mohawks were refused service at gas stations and were turned away from restaurant after restaurant, finally able to secure food only through the back door of an establishment.

"Never mind all that," Mr. Jesse commanded his boys. "Never mind all that! We're here to play baseball. Baseball!"

And play they did. "We *whooped* 'em," Madison hollers.

"Yes sir," Lomax says, moved to contribute. "Whooped 'em good, 14 to 6."

"Pugh hit one clear out of the park," May says. "Clear *out* of old Pensacola stadium."

"And then," Pugh drawls. "And *then*, we turned around and whooped 'em again when they came here!"

"Whooped 'em worse," Emanuel joins in.

"That's right," Bennie Harris says.

"If I'm not mistaken," Ellis May says, raising his arms, presiding, "I *believe* the score was eight-teen," he says, pausing so others can give voice to their pride, then silencing them again, finishing in that quiet, "to two," holding up two lonely digits.

They would play the white Seagulls again that year for the championship. Though that game was tougher, and closer, they beat them again, for the third time in one season, winning the championship.

The culmination of the Mohawk year was later, in December. The city of Mobile, still governed by an all-white commission, created a special citizenship award to honor Mr. Jesse's efforts, as a leader in the community, an ambassador for the city wherever he went, and a levelheaded spokesman during those troubled times. They presented him the plaque when they awarded the championship trophy to the team.

Back at their clubhouse behind 1609 Bullshead Avenue, Jesse hoisted the trophy and the plaque before his team and told them, "*This*, gentlemen, your success, our success, is my dream come true." And then the big man broke down and cried.

Coaches Lomax and Emanuel hustled the players from the room but the chief called them back in. "It's all right, it's all right," he told them. "It's all right that they see a man crying, that they see a man *can* cry."

"I sure *loved* your daddy," Candyman says to Jesse.

"Shoot," Jack Tillman says. "*Everybody* loved your daddy."

Tillman, white, Mobile County sheriff, had gotten there late. At the time, he'd offered by way of apology, "Usually, when a black man tells you the show's at 1, you don't bother to show up till 2, or 3," to no one's offense. "Ain't that true, Jesse?" he asked.

"Whatever you say, Jack," Jesse answered, shaking his head and laughing at Jack just like the rest of them.

"I remember the first time I met your daddy. I was sitting around home out in Semmes and the phone rang. I answered, 'Hello?' This deep, raspy voice said, 'Speak to Jack Tillman.' I said, 'This is he.'

"'This is Jesse Norwood. I hear you got a baseball team,' this voice says.

"'Yes sir. That's right.'

"'When's your next game?'

"'Well, sir, we've had some trouble getting up games lately,' I tell him.

"'Why don't you come down to Trinity Gardens

and play my team?'

"Trinity Gardens? I'm thinking, Oh, sheeit."

The Mohawks, as is usually the case whenever Jack's around, are starting to lose control.

"I don't know, can you *sound* black on the telephone, Jesse?"

Jesse just keeps shaking his head, unable to answer, from laughing. So Jack turns to his dear old friend Emanuel and repeats the question, "Can you?"

"Hush up, Jack," Emanuel answers him.

"All right, all right. So I says, 'I don't know, Mr. Norwood. I've got to make some phone calls, see if I can get up a team.'

"'Be there eleven o'clock,' he tells me, and hangs up.

"We're talking *Trinity Gardens* in nineteen-sixty-five!" Jack says, prompting others to tell him to shut up, by which they really mean, get on with the story. But Jack, as they all know, tells his story his own way, does just about everything his own way. He would later become a professional boxer, the number-two ranked welterweight in the world. All the men in this room can easily recognize the pugilistic bent of his nature, had seen it early, and often. "The damn interstate doesn't even go all the way to Trinity Gardens in 1965!" he says.

"But I call everyone up and we meet at Bessemer, where I-65 ends, and then proceed on to Trinity Gardens. Eleven o'clock, and *nobody's* there!"

"That's right," Jesse says.

"We're starting to think, what in the hell is this, when along comes big ol' Jesse Norwood, and his team, and hundreds of fans, I mean *hundreds*.

"Jesse had cooked up some ribs, so we ate, drank a few beers, and then finally get around to baseball. We were going to play a doubleheader. I was going to pitch the first game, Beau Seales the second. Now I'm a pretty good pitcher at the time."

"You ain't lying," Emanuel says.

"I held the county strikeout record for twenty-seven years, struck out a hundred-and-sixty-something in eighteen games! I had some pop on my fastball, and a big ol' curve. I'm out there all cocky and such, in front of this *huge* crowd, and I strike out their first two batters. Isn't that right, Robert?"

Emanuel just glares at him.

"Then up comes ol' Sleepy. Now Sleepy's tall, like six-two, six-three, but he's affable, like a big, tall puppy. And he's been around a while," Jack says, standing, stretching to his full height of only five-ten, and then taking up a batter's stance there in the assembly hall. "I throw two fastballs right by him, whap, whap, and I'm thinking, 'Shoot, this old man...' So I dial up the curve, big ol' hook, and I lay it in there right on the lower inside part of the plate. Well ol' Sleepy reaches down and wallops the thing, I mean *wallops* it, WHOP," Jack says, imitating a swing. "Knocked that sucker, must have been four-hundred-and-fifty feet. You remember?" he asks Emanuel.

"I sure do."

"Man, I didn't know a baseball could be hit that far, but I knew we were in for a game. These ol' boys could hit a baseball," he says. "Who won that game, Robert? I can't really remember."

"The hell you can't. You got blasted."

Jack reaches over and claps Emanuel on the shoulder. "Ol' Robert's still mad about what happened in the second game. You want to tell him about that?"

"Nope."

"Ol' Robert here's pretty fast. He tell you that? What you run the hundred in Robert, 9.4?"

"Something like that."

"I mean *fast* fast. So I'm playing center in the second game, and Robert gets on with a double. The next man," Harris raises his hand, "that's right, Bennie, gets a single. Well I scoop up the ball and throw a BB in there and get Robert out at the plate."

Emanuel crosses his arms and turns sideways to Jack.

"But that's not all! Three innings later, Emanuel's on second again, and Bennie gets another hit, and off goes Robert, tearing around the bases. Well I scoop up that ball again," Jack says, getting back out of his chair, "and I throw another BB in there, and I get him a-gain!" Jack cries. "Twice! In one game!"

"Sit down, Jack," Emanuel says, pushing his friend to his seat.

"Oh, man, we had us some good times," Jack says.

"I bet we played sixty games against black teams the next year, loving every minute of it, loving every *second*!"

"Tell him about the Athletics game," Pugh says.

"Which Athletics game?"

"After you started pitching for us," Pugh tells him, reminding him, "Big O."

"Oh, sheeit, *that* Athletics game.

"There must-a been two *thousand* people watching that game. They overran the stands, stood four, five deep all the way around the outfield. We had to string a rope around the field. I'm pitching, and up comes Big O, Big oh my *gawd...*" Jack moans.

"Go on," Pugh says, grinning.

"He hit a ball of mine, I swear to God, it flew out of the park, soared over those people out there beyond the rope," Jack says.

"I didn't take one step on it," Emanuel says. "Not one."

"That sucker went even *farther* than Sleepy's blast. You couldn't even *see* it, it went so far. Had to be five hundred feet, if it was an inch!"

The rest of the players laugh along with Jack, clap their hands.

"Am I lying, Jesse?" he asks.

"No, Jack, you aren't," Jesse tells him.

"Man, that was fun. I *loved* playing for your daddy. And we *never* had any problems, never had any race problems, black, white: Nobody *cared*! We were just playing baseball." Then he turns, and says, "Listen, Jesse's daddy took a skinny white kid from Semmes and let him play with the best, the *best*. He was a great, great man." To Jesse, he adds, "I shore miss your daddy."

"We all miss him, Jack," Jesse says, as the others murmur assent.

"This *community* misses him," Councilman Richardson says.

The men in the room, politicians, preachers, coaches, teachers, supervisors, executives, businessmen, even a token sheriff, all agree on that point, every one of them. They don't feel slighted in their efforts at the acknowledgment of Jesse's singular impact, not slighted at all. While they might aspire to similar appraisal, they know that in the big game that Jesse played, they haven't quite earned it yet. They know, from their time as Mohawks, from their baseball experience, that it's a long, continuous, cooperative effort. They didn't have superstars on the Mohawks, and Jesse didn't run the team like an autocrat. Every one contributed, in every facet of the organization. That is the true beauty of their organization, and the game, and why it was such a perfect vehicle for their salvation, deliverance, and growth.

A month before he was assassinated, Martin Luther King Jr. gave a sermon at Ebenezer Baptist Church on the drum-major instinct. "Before we judge ambitious disciples for their egotism," King said, "let us realize that we all have the drum-major instinct, the drive for recognition, distinction, specialness, to lead the parade, to be first. But if unmanaged, undisciplined, the drum-major instinct was pernicious; it distorted and degraded one's personality, one's soul. Runaway egotism spawned a host of sins, including corruption, criminality, exploitation, dishonesty, and exclusion. On a larger scale it led to prejudice and racism, and to powerful nations' lust to rule the world."[129]

And then he turned to Scripture, Jesus' "new definition of greatness," and "new norm for nobility." Jesus, King told the gathering, "said to James and John, 'You must earn it. True greatness comes not by favoritism, but by fitness,'"[130] fitness to contribute, serve.

And if the measure of greatness is servanthood, anyone could be great, because everyone can serve. "All one needed was 'a heart full of grace, a soul generated by love.' Long before and after Jesus, prophets and philosophers have been trying to reconcile the fullest individuality with the most just community. Greatness of servanthood may have been as good an answer as any ever found. The best woman or man was the one who did the most for the community."[131]

By that measure then, there can be no debate, not in this room, not in this community, about the magnitude of Jesse Norwood's impact on the lives of the men collected here, or the lives that orbit around their lives. They have managed to continue his efforts and his influence, but in the beginning it was just Jesse Norwood, just as in that other, brighter, more public galaxy it was just Jackie Robinson. The lesson to be learned from either, though, is that it's not necessary to be the first, or even the best. Because it's not the vastness of what they accomplished that counts. It's that they were willing to stand up and take on the task.

The question that has to be asked is not who was the greatest, or who did the most. The more pertinent question now, at this juncture thirty years later, when there is still so much unfinished business and still so much need, is how did Jesse Norwood do it at all, how did he *know*?

Jesse Jr. just shakes his head, says, "I don't know."

Jackie Robinson says he'd been an athlete all his life, was always playing games in the street, trying to be the best. And he had brother Mack to emulate, compete against, and learn from. Martin Luther King Jr. grew up in the church, was groomed for his ministry from day one, as was James Baldwin. Jesse Norwood had none of that, beyond constantly recognizing necessity and tackling it with whatever few tools he possessed.

Baldwin, like DuBois, emigrated from his homeland, unable to reconcile his "twoness," to Paris, where he wrote some of his best work. King wrestled with his calling continuously, suffered despair and depression, over what he regularly perceived as the ineffectualness of his work. That he maintained that effort to the bitter, tragic end is the measure of his character. In King's own words, distilling those efforts down to their most elemental motivating principle, he had tried, he said, "to love and serve humanity." Those words are part of the same drum-major instinct sermon delivered a month before his death, words that were dramatically re-aired in Ebenezer Baptist Church for his eulogy. In the dedication to *Let the Trumpet Sound*, Stephen B. Oates writes, "To the memory of Addie Mae Collins, Denise McNair, Carol Robertson, and Cynthia Wesley," the four girls killed in the Sixteenth Street Church bombing. "For it was to restore the beloved community, so that the children of the world might inherit a legacy of Peace, that he came down out of the academy, down from the pulpit, and marched his way to Glory."[132]

Loving and serving humanity, its children, its community: Looking around the room at this community of men, you can easily catch glimpses of those "little bitty babies" from long ago, in their laughter, their teasing. "Jesse Norwood saved those kids," Jimmy Knight likes to say. But he preserved them too, something just as remarkable, and maybe something else only achievable through the model of baseball. It was necessary, after all, to paraphrase Roy Campanella, one of the first in line to follow Jackie Robinson across the color barrier, that there be a lot of little boy in a man who plays baseball.

Still, the question persists: How did he know all this?

But the question merely bounces back, like a bobbled fungo. These men either don't have an answer, don't want to venture a guess, or don't feel a need to answer such a question. Finally, Sam Madison offers this:

"If you want your kid to grow, come to be a lady or a *gentleman*, you got to teach that kid early, right from wrong, faith in God," he says. "And how do you teach them that, how do you get them to listen to you? By giving them what they want the most."

Sam sits back, and waits, waits until everyone in the room is hanging on his answer, anticipating what that most wanted thing is. "Love," he allows at last, "And Mr. Jesse? He was all about love."

David Falkner tells a story in the very beginning of his book on Jackie Robinson, of what he calls that "epochal" game on August 29, 1947, where Robinson, mere months into his major league career, "had stolen home, had dismantled that invisible barrier confronting base runners of any size, shape, or color standing at third base; he had dismantled it as he had only months before dismantled a century of bigotry that had seemingly permanently sealed America's Pastime." Falkner continues, "A reporter that night went

to Branch Rickey, the architect of this greater dismantling, to ask him about the smaller one that had just
taken place on the field.

"'Who taught him to do things like that?' the
reporter inquired.

"'Primarily God,' Mr. Rickey answered."[133]

Eight

*J*ackie, of course, would have given an entirely different answer to that reporter's question. His answer would refer to the particular task, of stealing home. Counting the time it took for the pitcher's delivery against the number of steps he needed to cover the ninety feet from third to home, Jackie was, as Falkner states, "just doing what it took to get the job done."[134]

At the time, Jackie's job was baseball, but the successful application of his unique skills—such as the dismantling of the barrier confronting *any* runner on third, at will, seemingly at ease—determined the success of a greater dismantling, the segregation of all baseball, and the still greater dismantling of society at large, at a time when baseball represented and reflected that larger society in so many ways. And yet despite his successes, his personal, baseball success, and the intermediate success of the desegregation of baseball, in September of 1959, when the last all-white major league team, the Boston Red Sox, fielded its first African-American player, Pumpsie Green, the public high schools in Little Rock, Arkansas, were closed and empty, padlocked by a governor who vowed to *never* yield to federally mandated integration.

Baseball Has Done It, Jackie titled his 1964 book about the integration of the game. "Integration has already proved that all America can live together in peaceful competition,"[135] Jackie writes, posing the question, in essence: Baseball has done it, now what?

The book chronicles not only the successes of his and Rickey's "noble experiment," but also many desultory tales of the grip of prejudice and racism in and around the game regardless of the developments on the field of play. Racism reared its totem in everything from off-field accommodations, to pay scale, to opportunity for promotion into organizational hierarchy. It is bittersweet that the total commitment of black America to integration, which contributed directly to the abandonment and demise of the Negro Leagues by 1960, created a situation where *fewer* blacks were making a living playing baseball than there had been at any other time in the century, or so supposed Charles Einstein. "The side effects of integration included the destruction of a significant cultural entity and way of life. At one time the Negro Leagues had constituted one of the largest primarily black-owned and operated enterprises in the nation."[136]

Democracy killed Negro baseball, Tygiel quotes

Wendell Smith concluding. "The big league doors opened one day and when Negro players walked in, Negro baseball walked out."[137]

And yet there still existed places like Little Rock, Oxford, Albany, and Birmingham. It was not misguided, then, for Jesse Norwood to insist repeatedly that his Mohawks resist the impulse toward frustration and indignation, and just play baseball. For, indeed, Jackson, Mississippi, still existed. It would have been more misguided for Jesse to expend energy beyond baseball, at the time, futile for him to have argued with that white sheriff-umpire in any other terms than baseball. "We're here to play baseball" was his only appeal, even faced with the threat of jail, at a time, in a place, where defying a white sheriff could *easily* result in a jail sentence, or worse. Black men could easily disappear, only to be fished out of some river three days later, for far less offense than that. "Call a fair game or we'll leave."

It is further to Jesse Norwood's credit that he exhibited such restraint and restricted his efforts to the ball club. He considered himself a simple, modest man, not great at all, merely someone who recognized a need, and, like Jackie, was just trying to do whatever it took to get the job done. To him, that would be task enough, because it would be anything but easy, and it would require the kind of determined innovation only an Edison or a Franklin could appreciate.

"Oh, you should have *seen* some of the things we

used to do that job," Ellis May says, shaking his head in wonderment.

"Dirt skiing," Jesse says, grinning, nodding along.

"Say what?" Tillman asks.

"You remember?" Jesse says to the other players.

"Oh yeah," some answer.

"I remember as a boy, going to the ballpark, and you know how we smoothed out the infield? My father would chain a railroad cross-tie to the back of his station wagon and drag it across the infield."

"That's right," some of them say.

"But that's not all," Jesse says. "He used to have us little boys *stand* on the cross-ties, give them extra weight as he drove back and forth."

"Dirt skiing," Jack says.

"Exactly."

Then they talk about rehab and conditioning equipment.

"We didn't have no barbells," Candyman says. "There was no money for such as that. We had rocks, concrete, fence posts."

They ran the railroad tracks for balance and endurance.

"Pitchers ran *all* the time," Theodore Sellers says. "All the time."

"Oh, boy, did they," Pugh sighs, sounding thankful, all these years later, that he wasn't a pitcher.

"You know why, don't you?" Candyman asks. "Where do pitchers get tired first?"

"Their legs?"

"*That's* right, their legs. Mr. Jesse read that in a book too. And sore arms? Forget it. We never had sore arms."

"Lord, no," Reverend Emanuel says. "We were all the time *turning the wheel*."

"That's right," their president says again.

The wheel was an old bicycle rim, bolted through the hub to the wall just tight enough to give resistance against rotating it. Along the rim a spool was bolted on as a handle. The players sat and turned the wheel, every day, "Building up our tissues," May says.

"Now where in the Sam Hill did he come up with that?" Tillman asks, someone who had access to gyms and weight rooms.

"I don't know," Jesse Jr. says, shrugging, almost apologizing.

"We *made* them," Candyman says.

"I *know* that," Jack tells him. "Where did he come up with that idea?"

"He just did. *Whatever* it took. Injuries? Forget it. Third-degree burns? You get you a strawberry or something? Get you some dirt and some spit, rub it in there, get back out on the ball field."

"Oh, man," Pugh says. "I was all the time getting those strawberries, sliding on that hard dirt."

"Sprained ankle? Get some clay, clover, and water, mix it up, put it on. Three days later the swelling's down, you back in the game."

"Clover?"

"That's right, clo-ver. And if you cut yourself, need stitches, you think you going to the doctor?"

"No, no, no," Pugh says.

"No, sir. Spiderwebs."

"Spiderwebs?"

"You see this here?" May says, pointing to a scar on his left temple. "I got beaned one time by Mr. Sellers in practice. Thought I was going to lose an eye."

"Spiderwebs?"

"That's right."

"You should a learned how to hit," Pugh tells him.

"Mr. Secretary!" Candyman calls.

"Oh, Sweet," Madison says.

"Damn," Tillman says. "No wonder you boys was so tough."

"Whatever it took," Candyman tells him. "Whatever it took."

Whatever it took to play the game, because the game was their salvation. And Jesse Norwood made sure nothing, not injury, lack of resources or equipment, not even discrimination, got in the way of the baseball.

Jimmy Knight starts to tell a story of another, earlier visit to Pensacola, a night game, with a big pot of money at stake. It was a holiday tournament, over July 4th weekend, in '61, or '62, and his Hillsdale club had been involved.

"Oh, yeah," Madison says, remembering. "Lord

have mercy."

It came down to, as usual, a finale between the Seagulls and the Mohawks, when the umpire started trying to ensure a Pensacola victory.

"This was a real umpire too," Jimmy says. "These were serious games, with huge crowds."

Jesse took about all he could before he got up, said, "That's it. Let's go."

"Man says to Mr. Jesse, 'I ain't gonna pay your money.'

"Jesse says, 'I don't care. Keep it. Pack it up gentlemen.'"

"We had the stuff *in* the vans, getting ready to go," May says, "when they say, 'Come on and play. We'll play right.'

"They play the game right and we whoop 'em," he says. "Then they want to know, 'Where you boys from?'" Candyman pauses before saying, "Prichard."

But it's no wonder they wouldn't have known where Prichard was, or anything about it. There wasn't much to tell, beyond the Mohawks. The interstate hadn't made it to Prichard, so not much by way of industry had found its way out there either. The area was mostly pasture land, or farmland. Most boys could only find work picking cotton or potatoes or pulling corn. The only real, steady work to be had was down on the waterfront, if you were lucky to get picked from the pool of workers who showed up every morning, as a domestic in some white household, or out at Brookley Field, where Jesse Norwood had worked since the end of the war.

But then when Brookley closed down in 1962, it was felt in Prichard especially hard.

"Mr. Jesse had gotten me a job out at Brookley," Pugh says. "Now I'm out of work."

Sam Jones says lots of folks moved from Prichard after the base closed down, chasing work to New Orleans, Texas. "Not Jesse Norwood," he says. He stayed. Over halfway to retirement, the team he had devoted most of the last decade of his life to now successful and recognized, his boys on the brink of manhood, he stayed, despite the support that had allowed for so much of that endeavor disappearing beneath him. But now what?

Indeed, now what? Baseball was integrated. That process proved that black and white America could coexist and compete on the same field. Jackie Robinson was proof of that, and in fact would be inducted into the Baseball Hall of Fame in Cooperstown, New York, that fall. But at the same time, Martin Luther King Jr.'s efforts to desegregate Albany, Georgia, had bogged down, would come to be viewed as a failure of his nonviolent strategy, fracturing the movement. King's Southern Christian Leadership Council, the Student Nonviolent Coordinating Committee, and Roy Wilkins's NAACP—which DuBois had helped charter decades earlier and Jackie Robinson figured prominently in—all struggled with increasingly diverging strategies toward reaching the overall goal of racial equality.

King had been outmaneuvered in Albany, with Sheriff Laurie Pritchett peacefully arresting the demonstrators and jailing them in several counties, wherever he could find cells. King ran out of marchers before Pritchett ran out of jail space.

The SNCC was advocating a more confrontational, even radical approach. It had started two years earlier at that Woolworth's lunch counter in North Carolina, the students defying local ordinances and willingly going to jail to draw attention to their cause. It was a direct, grassroots strategy, confronting segregation practices face-to-face. And when those students were arrested, the person they appealed to for guidance and support was not Wilkins or King but Jackie Robinson. Jackie corresponded with the jailed protestors, maybe recalling how he'd led those Black Panthers in his battalion in similar protests at lunch counters in the base town outside of Fort Hood, or the dispute over seating in the canteen at Fort Riley. And then he staged an "Afternoon of Jazz" concert on the grounds of his Connecticut home, what would become an annual event, a fundraiser for the students in North Carolina.

Almost from the beginning of his involvement with the civil rights movement, Jackie realized the importance of economic activism as well as political. Even before his playing days were over, in 1951, he'd opened up a short-lived clothing store in Harlem. The success of baseball's integration notwithstanding, peaceful cooperation wouldn't work on a broad enough level without economic independence. That has always been true. It was economic disparity that forced that first black baseball league, the League of Colored Base Ball Clubs, to shut down. Who can say what difference it might have made in all aspects of this story, if those teams had survived? If professional major league teams promoted players on merit all along, from black and white affiliates, what might we be saying today about Satchel Paige, or Josh Gibson, James Harris, Moose Andrews, Sleepy Burns, or Shoe Lomax? Michael Lomax suggests that if more black baseball teams in late-nineteenth-century America had owned their own ballparks, rather than entering into dubious lease agreements with their white counterparts because of political restrictions against that ownership, they might have been able to capitalize on the early baseball craze and might have been able to survive.

In his first spring out of baseball, 1957, Jackie traveled the country raising money for the NAACP's Freedom Fund. And in that initial campaign the Fund passed the million-dollar donation mark for the first time. It proved to Jackie that people were indeed willing to pay for their freedom, were willing to sacrifice, if the organizers could but get their story told. At the organization's year-end convention Jackie gave his closing address on the need for sacrifice, on everyone's part. In his post-baseball years he became increasingly aware that there were two keys to the advancement of America's blacks, and they were, as he told Al Duckett, the ballot and the buck.

In January of 1958 he was named to the board of directors of the NAACP and at the same time invited to Jackson, Mississippi, by Medgar Evers, to commemorate Jackie Robinson Day, February 16 of that year. He attended the celebration and spoke to a large crowd in a Masonic temple in Jackson surrounded by angry whites and Mississippi state police, a situation reminiscent of the one the Mohawks found themselves in a year later, and a harbinger of how the struggle for civil rights would be contested, not commercially, not politically, and certainly not competitively, but violently. Jackie had heard a broadcast of the Monitor radio network on his way to the rally and he told his audience about it. It was an interview with a Klan member, a minister, who said he would *never* let his children attend an integrated school. Asked what he would do about it, that man of God explained, "he had two guns, ammunition, and enough money to buy more guns."[138]

It would come down to violence, in the streets of Birmingham, on a bridge in Selma, in the Mississippi delta and the ghettos of Los Angeles, and Baltimore, and Rochester, to move enough of America to hear the story and bring about a change: violence, not time, a fact of the matter that both Robinson and King increasingly acknowledged, and ultimately suffered from.

It may be true, as Roger Kahn suggests in *Games We Used to Play*, that baseball reflects light; it does not originate it—the difference between the moon and the sun—that the illuminating success of Jackie Robinson did not shine beyond the confines of the ballpark, did not shed any light upon the hatred in some men's souls, but Jesse Norwood refused to believe it. In 1962, when Brookley Field closed, Jesse Norwood stayed in Prichard, kept the Mohawks together. Baseball was still a highlight of Mobile sports, with Jones and Agee and Otis poised to step onto center stage. And his Mohawks were becoming the hottest of teams. Jesse went into business for himself, buying his first Esso station, becoming the first independent black business owner in the city.

"He knew that individual economic development was the foundation for change in the black community," Commissioner Jones says. "He created jobs and revenue, pure and simple."

Most of the original Mohawks, out of high school by the time, stayed with the team. Jesse subsidized some of them, put others to work for him, even paid for someone like Emanuel to come home from college on summer weekends so he could play ball. The Mohawks, and baseball, became the central concern of his life, for he saw what it had done for those boys, saw how baseball had helped them navigate through the darkness, saw them now, as young men, reaching out and helping other boys find their way too.

"Oh, yeah," Pugh will allow, "we was already helping other kids."

"Groomed ol' Popcorn here," Madison says, jerking a thumb over his shoulder toward the back of the room.

Fatherless, like many of them, "Popcorn" Campbell didn't want to talk much about baseball when he was interviewed separately. He deferred most questions to others. "You'll have to ask Mr. Sleepy about that," he'd say. Or, "Mr. Candyman probably knows the answer to that." He is a handsome man, who has kept himself in shape. He's quick with his bright, easy smile. He just doesn't talk much. He would grumble from time to time—"Oh, man, not *Syracuse*"—though he would never really say why. He perked up when there was mention of a possible exhibition game with the university team, ready to pitch. But beyond that, all he would definitively allow was, "Mr. Jesse *raised* me," which means, mostly, that in a world where he was almost completely invisible, Jesse Norwood saw him and attended to his needs.

"Aw, we did that for all the Apaches," Pugh says, bringing that smile to Campbell's face. "Cut their hair, shined their shoes, got them to school," he lists.

"That's how Remerick got his start," Jimmy Knight says. A barbershop owner in town, Jimmy, somewhat mystified, had said that Remerick made upwards of ten thousand dollars more a year than he did, as a county board of education superintendent. "But he says he owes it all to his time as a Mohawk, with Jesse Norwood," Knight added.

"We taught them the fundamentals," May says of the Apaches, steering the discussion back to baseball. "Used to teach them the same drills we practiced, from the same books"; they taught them how to execute a double-play from the same book by Pee Wee and Junior. "'Is that what it says in the book?' we'd ask."

"Cause we loved them," Madison adds, "like Mr. Jesse loved us, we taught them to love baseball."

Pugh sits up straighter in his chair at that comment, says, "Shoot, Bo, you taught them to love *a* baseball, that's what you did."

Madison grins at the accusation.

After a few moments, Jimmy Knight asks, "What do you mean, Lyonel?"

"Shoot," he says again. "Bo had a scam going with those boys."

"You just jealous," Sam says, still grinning.

Jesse had long ago incorporated the practice of compensating kids at Mohawk Park for retrieving and returning foul balls or home runs hit into the woods or the cornfield. Baseballs would always be precious commodities. They say that the famous McCovey shift originated in Mobile, because of the scarcity of baseballs, not as a defensive strategy. In the big leagues, it's estimated that the life span of a baseball is five to seven pitches. At that rate, fifty, sixty, a hundred or more might be put into play over the course of nine innings. Back on the sandlots of Mobile, five to seven baseballs would have to last teams like the Mohawks for weeks, even months. That's the truth behind the supposition that had there been more baseballs, there would have been more baseball played, more baseball players. When they couldn't convince McCovey to bat right-handed, diminishing his power enough to at least keep the batted ball in sight, they stacked the right side of the field against his left-handed blasts to have a player somewhere in the vicinity of his 400- and 500-foot shots.

While Jesse didn't charge admission to their games in Trinity Gardens—he passed his hat through the crowds instead, asking for only what they could afford to contribute—he did pay those kids for returning the precious items.

"Get that ball!" he'd holler out any time a home run or foul ball was hit to the right side, into the woods.

By the early sixties the exchange rate was fifty cents for a new ball, twenty-five for used. At the time, it cost a quarter to get into the matinee cartoons on Saturday afternoon at the Saenger Theater in downtown Mobile.

"Sam Madison split the profits with them little kids!" Pugh charges.

Sam snickers at the memory. "They would come

up to me before a game and say, 'Mr. Sam, we want to go to the *show*," he says.

"Shoot, man," Pugh says a third time. "That's not what they meant, and you *know* it."

"Sure it is."

"Shoot."

"What I did was," Madison then confesses, "I'd tell them where to stand, where I'd hit the ball."

"We're talking fair *and* foul balls. I used to stand out by the foul pole and direct those kids to the ball," Pugh says. "For *free*!"

Madison's smile, turned snicker, grows into a full-throated chuckle, "Heh, heh, heh. One time, I fouled off about eight balls to those kids. Mr. Jesse caught on to what I was doing."

"*Every*body knew what you was doing!"

"He said to me, 'Bo, hit it straight this time.'"

"But did that stop him? No. He was making too much money. I look up, ready to point, and there's already four or five boys standing out there, waiting on the ball!"

"Helping 'em to the *show*," Madison says.

Jesse, Jimmy, the rest of them just shake their heads at the story. Jack Tillman turns to Madison and says, "You *rascal*."

"Heh, heh, heh."

Campbell, of all people, defends the practice. "Made good business sense."

"Shoot," Pugh says one last time, waving off both

Sam and Popcorn.

Campbell, though, must have gotten the skewed entrepreneurial message, from that experience, and the model that Jesse Norwood provided. He would, after his baseball days, go into business for himself, right there in Prichard.

At the same time, 1962, as the movement was failing in Albany, Brookley Field was closing, Jackie Robinson was being inducted into baseball's Hall of Fame. But that was the year Jackie suffered his first heart attack as well. The health of one of the greatest athletes the country has ever produced was beginning to fail though he was only forty-three years old.

In 1964, Jackie had a second, more serious heart attack. Circulatory problems, complications brought on by diabetes, diminished his gait and his eyesight. Amid the growing racial violence, where the mutilated bodies of three voting rights workers were dug out of a Mississippi swamp that August, a month after the most significant civil rights legislation in a century had been passed in Congress, and political failure—his highly criticized alignment with Richard Nixon and then Nelson Rockefeller, the defeat of the Mississippi Freedom Democratic Party at the party's nominating convention—Jackie turned his attention to the creation of a predominantly black-owned bank, the Freedom National Bank in Harlem, the nation's largest black-owned financial institution. "Long before other black leaders stressed the irreducible importance of economics in changing the racial land-scape," Falkner writes, "Robinson grasped its significance perfectly."[139]

Jesse Norwood opened a second gas station about that time, and he also became a regional promoter for a traveling rock-and-roll music revue. He would book shows and secure venues for concerts all over the southeast for the likes of Jackie Wilson, Marvin Gaye, Wilson Pickett, Otis Redding, Sam Cooke, and Little Stevie Wonder. He was the only black promoter in the region, for the largest such production company in the country. Some of his ballplayers were enfranchised in this venture too. In advance of the shows, he'd truck a station wagon full of Apaches to the towns and they'd plaster store windows and telephone poles with posters advertising upcoming events. He used his Mohawks as security and ushers during the shows. And he put Pugh back to work too.

"Yes, sir," he says. "I did a lot of the driving for Mr. Jesse." As they traveled the roads from Biloxi to Pensacola, Mobile to Montgomery, Jackson to Columbus, Pugh says, "Mr. Jesse would get so tired, he'd sleep in the car."

Jesse Norwood's health was on the verge of failing, too, as he placed more stress on his body, devoted more time to his businesses and baseball team. He had his sights set on life beyond baseball for these men. He'd seen the success of the team, the integration of

athletic events, of the Mohawks, with Jack Tillman.
He knew, as Jackie knew, that integration worked. But
even with the Civil Rights Act of 1964, and then the
Voting Rights Act a year later, opportunity had to be
articulated, exhibited. That's what he was focusing on.

"My father," Jesse Jr. says, "never intended to lead
the Mohawks forever. He only planned to bring the
organization to a certain level"—he holds his hand
about shoulder height—"and step aside. All along, his
plan was to take these men from where they were"—
sweeping that hand now to his far left—"to where
they needed to be," he says, holding up his other hand
to the far right, illustrating the physical, emotional,
and psychological distance traveled.

The men sit there, watch, and listen to Jesse,
politician, namesake of their chief, nodding their
heads silently, recalling the journey.

Jesse continues. "We used to accuse my father of
never finishing what he started. But I understand differently now, looking at these men. He wanted to get
them from here, to here," he says, framing the distance again, "and then step aside, to shift the responsibility from one man, to the community. That was the
only way it would *really* last."

Jesse goes on to say that his father never wanted
to be the Martin Luther King of Prichard, Alabama.
That's why he said he didn't want the story of the
Mohawks to be a story about his father. But in fact, so
many of his father's ideas and plans anticipate or echo

those of King's that it's hard *not* to associate the efforts of each to those of the other.

Martin Luther King Jr.'s "dream" personified would have been the realization of what he called a "beloved community," alluded to in Oates's dedication to *Let the Trumpet Sound.* The term had been coined after the Civil War by Harvard philosopher Josiah Royce, to describe a societal reformation brought about by what Gandhi would later call "soul-force." King had tried to use Gandhi's phrase, translated literally from the Sanskrit as "clinging" or "grasping" to "truth" or "love," as the descriptor of his movement— rather than passive resistance or nonviolence— though he couldn't make it stick. "*Soul force* was a good name for King's method because, like the satyagrahi, the soul-force activist in the American context sought to remold her personality in the course of struggle in such a way that her transformation and that of others would lead to society-wide transformation. What Hindus called the universal Soul and transcendentalists the Oversoul, King called the beloved community," Burns explains.[140]

That remolding came about only through self-respect and self-confidence, so that the activist could take up a stance of emphatic, redeeming goodwill, a "way of seeing and approaching the Other, a way of communicating," the "suspension of judgment and prejudice,"[141] in a word, love, though not in the tender, emotional, or romantic sense. Something more like *agape*, tough-love.

"That's the kind of love I'm talking about," Madison says.

And then Reverend Lomax makes one of his rare comments, "Tough like a lion, gentle as a lamb."

"Amen," his fellow reverend Emanuel says.

Toward the end of his book, Burns puts it this way: "King was convinced that assertive nonviolent action, which he liked to call soul force, was not only more ethical than violence but more effective, especially long term. He did not think that violent methods had ever been truly effective, whether in the Civil War, which left its legacy of wretched white supremacy, in global warfare, or in ghetto riots. In just six decades since its 'invention' by Gandhi in 1906, mass nonviolent action in King's view had proven more successful than six millennia of human violence. This was partly because it did not leave bitterness behind to haunt future generations. It stymied the law of the multiplication of evil"[142]—a multiplication factored by abuse, confrontation, retaliation, murder, and rioting. This soul-force was "the synthesis of justice and compassion, of faith and understanding, of social and personal rebirth," the "fire of faith and moral passion not only to break down the walls of inhumanity, but to forge the new person," what would, ultimately, deliver his "beloved community, knit together by compassionate understanding, heartfelt communication, bonds of human intimacy."[143]

*

"Love," Madison says.

That's where Jesse Norwood brought these men, this community, by the mid-1960s. And he brought them there, expressly, through baseball. There is no evidence to suggest that it is anything more than an inspired coincidence, but the vehicle he used to take those boys from being troubled youth, what Dyson calls today those "despised black youth,"[144] to responsible, loving men who, like him, would stay in Prichard and become leaders and spokesmen in their community—baseball—was the perfect vehicle for the task. Beyond being a showcase of how the races could compete and coexist together, at a more universal and elemental level, there is evidence that baseball is a model for that personal and social reformation essential for achieving King's "beloved community." In baseball, social scientist and philosopher George Herbert Meade finds the template for the socialization of children, the crucial step of their being able to take on the role of the Other, recognizing that there is an Other, realizing their place in a larger, multifarious community. More specifically, Meade sees the act of hitting a baseball as an exercise of taking on that role of the Other. The basic fundamental task of adjusting to a pitch, holding back on a curveball, swinging to an opposite field, shortening your stroke, is an acknowledgment of a wider collective. Hitting a baseball, that most difficult task of any sport, required, first, overcoming fear, according to Koppett, required a certain faith in ability, a self-assurance; it ingrained a recognition of the Other, fairly constituted a "beloved community." By 1967 the Mohawks seemed on the verge of achieving just that.

"I can give you proof of that," Jesse Jr. says. "Even as young as I was at the time, I remember noticing this. When a white team came to play the Mohawks in Trinity Gardens in those years, Jack's team, other white teams, the fans would start off like this," he says, holding his hands up again, in polarized opposition. "But by the seventh-inning stretch, say, they'd be like this," he says, interlacing the fingers of both hands together. "And that's a fact."

"We never had *any* problem," Jack says.

"No. And here's another fact: If any police *did* show up, it was only because he wanted to watch the game!"

"Damn right," Tillman the sheriff says.

"These guys *changed* the community. We didn't have any street gangs, or bullies, or drugs because of these guys walking around in their Mohawk caps and Mohawk jackets."

"I remember going to his shows down at the auditorium, seeing the Four Tops or Chuck Berry," Tillman goes on. "There'd be twelve thousand people in the audience, half black, half white. There was *never* any problems."

"Because of these guys," Jesse says again.

And yet, in other cities across the nation, ghettos were aflame, in Watts, Detroit, and Newark. Across the ocean, Buddhist monks were immolating themselves protesting the Vietnam War. When it became evident that the legislative acts of recent years would not dent racism and poverty, King "grasped that 'civil rights' carried too much baggage of the dominant tradition of American individualism and not enough counterweight from a tradition of communitarian impulses, collective striving, and common good."[145]

He recognized that "the polar strains of individualism and collectivism needed to be reconciled, as he strove to reconcile other opposites."[146]

He even came to embrace "Black Power's celebration of black pride and racial identity," citing it in the last book he would author, *Where Do We Go from Here*, published in the spring of 1967, as "the latest manifestation of a centuries-old struggle by black people to reconcile their African past with their American present and future."[147]

But by that time, what with the increasing violence and militancy, King was "alarmed now that the two poles of liberation, personal and structural, were shooting off in opposite directions."[148]

As he "surveyed the shattered landscape of the summer of 1967, the summer of love and hate, he agonized not only about broken promises, his and others, but about all the centrifugal forces pulling the society apart. Chaos was drowning community. After all the movement's trials and triumphs over the past decade, how could so many alienated youth of all colors hold such shallow understandings of freedom? How had he contributed to this tragic misunderstanding?"[149]

How, after a decade's worth of so much effort and so much work, could King have arrived at a point where he was questioning that work, viewing it in terms of failure? Where *do* we go from there, a place King recognized as the end of civil rights and the beginning of black liberation, from the beloved community to somewhere as radical and extreme as Moses Fleetwood Walker's New Liberia? Had the visions of Gandhi and Walker, contemporaries but polar opposites, really borne out Walker's resignation that there was "nothing but failure and disappointment for the Negro in America"?

In his "Christmas Sermon on Peace," broadcast on Christmas Eve of 1967 over the Canadian Broadcasting System, "King acknowledged 'that not long after talking about' the dream in Washington, 'I started seeing it turn into a nightmare.' He spoke of the nightmarish conditions of Birmingham, where four girls were murdered in a church bombing a few weeks after his speech. He spoke of the punishing poverty that he observed in the nation's ghettoes as the antithesis of his dream, as were the race riots and the Vietnam War. King confessed that while 'I am personally the victim of deferred dreams, of blasted hopes,' that 'I still have a dream,'"[150] he insisted, though he had only a hundred nights left in which to dream, before he was assassinated by James Earl Ray.

Exactly a month before that bullet silenced King, Jackie Robinson's private world blew apart, with the arrest of his son, Jackie Jr., at 2:15 in the morning on a street corner in Stamford, Connecticut, in possession of heroin, marijuana, and a .22 caliber pistol. Young Jackie, who had struggled mightily to find himself within the shadow of his famous father, had found only drug addiction, crime, and deceit.

"It's a funny thing," Melvin Norwood might have said about that whole dynamic. Firstborn Norwood son, he was passed over for the bequeathing of his father's Christian name.

Second son, Jesse Jr., admits, "I don't know why he did that," sounding apologetic, almost. "I do know that he would single me out for instruction. I remember clearly, when we'd be sitting around watching television or something, him pulling me aside, saying 'Look at this,' or 'Think about this.'"

It's quite probable, Jesse will allow, that his father was grooming him to step into his shoes all those years, just as he'd groomed Ellis May to be the administrator of the team, its president, and groomed Lyonel Pugh to be a coach within the system, a businessman without. But by 1968, when the chief suffered his first heart attack and had to back off all that he was involved with, when the team started to falter, Jesse was not quite old enough to take on that responsibility, nor was he especially inclined to try. He had fought his own battle for recognition, as a junior, and veered away from the game, further admitting, "I didn't *want* to play baseball"—not after all those years of being obligated to attend the games only to be relegated to the sidelines like any other fan.

"I do remember feeling, at the time, that he paid a whole lot more attention to the team than he did his own family, his own children. So sure, yeah, there was probably a purpose to my not getting involved with it. I probably could have done more to keep it going. I faulted him, at the time, when in retrospect…"

The Mohawks watch Jesse's wrestling with those truths, listen to his confession with their customary respect and compassion. Reverend Lomax, standing beside Jesse, finally speaks into the ensuing silence. "A lot of us *tried* to keep it going." Lomax was the one Mr. Jesse had confided in after the heart attack that he didn't think he was going to be around much longer.

Sleepy tried to guide the team in Mr. Jesse's absence. Albert Lomax had moved from the area with his business, and the elder Emanuel was too busy with his to take on more duties with the team. His own health problems, a bad knee, for one, limited Sleepy's effectiveness.

Ellis May had already drifted away from the team, and while Pugh hung on for another year or so, he says, "I really didn't want to play for anyone else," other than Mr. Jesse.

Madison is quiet. He had gone from his encounter with that Athletics scout a year earlier, and his perceived failure, into the army, for a tour in the war that Walter Cronkite pronounced that summer of 1968 as "unwinnable." That experience could only have exacerbated Sam's feelings of inadequacy and failure, as he found himself on a twenty-year binge in an attempt to drown out those and any other feelings.

Campbell is quiet too, militantly quiet. He refused to discuss those last years, to the extent of deliberately evading the subject by claiming that he didn't really remember.

Sam Jones would say in another venue, though, that James "Popcorn" Campbell took Jesse Norwood's death two years later harder than anyone else. "Anyone."

By the time of Jesse's death in 1970, the Mohawks team was all but dead, as was semipro baseball in Mobile in general.

"You've got to remember," Jimmy Knight says, "how important and influential this team was. Not only did those other teams look forward to playing the Mohawks, they imitated the Mohawks, they *worked* to be compared to the Mohawks."

There were other factors in the demise of baseball, he'll allow. "Those were troubled times," he says. When he's asked, pointedly, what he *thinks* was the most significant factor undermining the game, he answers, "Drugs. Drugs came into the neighborhoods, captured the attention of those youth." Jimmy goes on to say that he doesn't know, had Jesse Norwood lived longer, if even he would have been able to compete in that arena, whether he could have combated that societal and municipal failure.

"Oh, I don't know," Sheriff Tillman muses. "You'd be surprised the difference one good man can make."

The others don't argue. Jimmy says only, "That's true."

Responding to the strife of the times, Jackie Robinson is on record as saying, in the aftermath of Robert Kennedy's murder that June, that "American society, whose white rulers spend so much time cautioning black people to be nonviolent, is one of the most violent civilizations on the map. And the rest of the world knows it." Robinson was speaking as a frightened father as much as a concerned citizen or political spokesman. "Everything he feared most seemed to be converging all at once: his son was fighting drug addiction, the civil rights leader he most believed in had been slain, cities were in flames across the country, and the candidate who had cost him so much credibility was marching to the White House."[151]

Mostly, as Falkner states, Jackie feared the recognition that he had somehow failed himself, as a father. "'I guess I had more of an effect on other people's kids than I had on my own' was all Robinson could bring himself to say to reporters"[152] after his son's arrest.

"What you've got to understand," Jesse Norwood Jr., says, "what Jimmy Knight has to understand, what *everyone* has to understand, is that the single most important thing my father did for those boys was that he *never* let them fail." We were sitting at a table in a glassed-in conference room of the Toulminville Public Library, a softball's toss from where Ed Scott "discovered" young Henry Aaron, just the two of us.

Jesse paused a moment to let the import of that statement sink in. "He didn't promise them success, that they'd become professional ballplayers. He didn't *give* them anything they didn't work for. He set out to do everything possible to ensure that those boys out there in that street in front of his house would not, ultimately, fail. The same as he did for me," added Jesse, who's had considerable success, as a student, an athlete, a politician, and now a community activist and businessman.

As the former mayor of Prichard, in fact, Jesse knew, "That's the message, a strong, lifelong message, that isn't getting to today's kids. We got babies— babies no older than those boys were—who have never gotten that message, having babies. There's a whole generation growing up amongst nothing *but* failure."

Sam Madison is a testimony to the strength of that message. In 1987, he found himself at the University of South Alabama Medical Center, across the street from the Toulminville branch library.

"I sat on that curb for two hours, not knowing what I should do. I only knew that I couldn't keep doing what I was," he says, of his drinking. "I sat there searching, for hours, with Mr. Jesse's teachings flaring up in my mind. 'You just aren't in the right place, Bo,' I heard him saying to me. So I said, All right. I'll put myself in a better place. I'll put myself in God's hands," he says, holding his out. He got up off the curb and entered the hospital's rehab facility and emerged weeks later clean, sober, a changed man, but not a complete man. "No," he cautions any presumptions along those lines. "I have a lot of debate with myself," he says, on the subject. "But I'm *still* working to become the man Mr. Jesse Norwood saw in that clubhouse behind 1609 Bullshead forty-five years ago." More than any of the others, perhaps, Madison wishes the elder Norwood could have been there to witness how they'd all turned out.

Jackie Robinson, on the other hand, was lucky, he says, to witness the return and rehabilitation of his son, Jackie Jr. He was fortunate to be able to reestablish their relationship, if only briefly. Jackie tells a story of the culminating moment of that return, at the end of a picnic he and his wife, Rachel, had given at their home for the staff of the Daytop drug addiction treatment center where young Jackie had finally freed himself from the grip of drugs and then become part of the staff:

"When Jackie had left home to go into the service, we drove him to the train and I suppose I had the thoughts any father has watching his son leave for service. I was proud of him and I was concerned because I knew quite well there was a chance he might never come back. I was worried because I knew that telling him good-bye was rough for Rachel. As he was about to leave us, Rachel reached out and took him in her arms in a loving hug. Impulsively, I wanted to do the same thing. But just as I raised my arms to embrace him, his hand shot up and stopped me, and he took my hand in his in a firm handclasp. In our unspoken language, I knew that the love was there but what he was telling me was that men don't embrace. And I understood. That had been several years ago…

"Now on the lawn of our home, on the evening of the picnic, our confused and lost kid who had gone off to war, who had experienced as much life in a few short and turbulent years as many never do in a life-time, that same kid had now become a young man, growing in self-esteem, growing in confidence, learning about life, and learning about the massive power of love. He stood in front of us, the last on that line of thankful guests, and reached out and grabbed Rachel and hugged her to him. His gratitude and appreciation were a tremendous sight. I stuck out my hand to shake his hand, remembering the day of his departure for the service. He brushed my hand aside, pulled me to him, and embraced me in a tight hug.

"That single moment paid for every bit of sacrifice, every bit of anguish, I had ever undergone.

"I had my son back."[153]

Junior had been clean for three years, had testified before the United States Senate Sub-Committee to Investigate Juvenile Delinquency on October 30, 1970, about the devastating, pernicious influence of drugs on the day's youth. There to speak of his experiences as a former victim of that influence, he was also on the front line in the battle to combat it. He worked at Daytop. He lectured youth groups frequently. And he was solely responsible for the planning the twelfth annual Afternoon of Jazz at his parents home, an event conceived to support the nascent Student Nonviolent Coordinating Committee all those years earlier. The proceeds from that year's event would go to help fund Daytop. But Jackie Robinson Jr. was killed in an automobile accident on June 17, 1971.

On the preceding Sunday morning he gave a talk to the congregation of the Nazarene Congregational Church in Bedford-Stuyvesant about that very same drug menace. He talked bluntly about his addiction, the crimes he had committed to support those habits, the difficult time at Daytop to kick them, but mostly he talked about his father, drawing a parallel to the story of the prodigal son.

He said he was "haunted by the image of being the son of a father who was a great man. So when I found I couldn't deal with him as a man and found that my father couldn't identify with me as his son, I stopped trying to find a man who wasn't there. I tried to eliminate the desire that I thought would never be fulfilled." He retreated instead into addiction.

"Daytop," he said, "helped me through discipline to find the father I had lost."

And then in concluding, much like the prodigal son, he said, "My father was always in my corner. I didn't always recognize that and I didn't always call on him, but he was always there."[154]

Six days after Jackie Jr.'s funeral, they held the jazz festival. It was a great success, Jackie says, but what stands out in friend Evelyn Cunningham's memory of the event is how Jackie conducted himself as gracious yet bereaved host. "Yes I am Jackie Robinson," she characterizes his attitude on that day, as she watched in amazement while he greeted and conversed with nearly all of the hundreds in attendance. "I am famous, it's been hell for me, but so what, let me give something back of myself."[155]

Sixteen months later, Jackie Robinson, all but blind, and lame, his hair completely white, only fifty-three years old, suffered a massive heart attack at his home and died in the ambulance on the way to the hospital.

"A life is marked by two dates with a dash in between," principal eulogist Jesse Jackson said in his remarks at Jackie's funeral. "It is in that dash, between those dates, where we live. For everyone," he said, his preacher's cadence catching the crowd, "there is a dash of possibility, to choose the high road or the low road, to make things better or make things worse."[156]

Jackie Robinson made things better, for everyone.

Nine days earlier, even if he had long ago ceased to function as a trail-blazing pioneer, he was still pointing the way along the path to a better place, a right place. At a major league baseball game in Cincinnati, Ohio, commemorating the twenty-fifth anniversary of his debut with the Dodgers, Robinson told the crowd he was pleased to be so honored. "But I will be more pleased the day I can look over at the third-base line and see a black man as manager."[157]

Manager Jesse Norwood, of the Prichard Mohawks, shared Jackie Robinson's vision and hope. He incorporated the promise of Jackie Robinson and the model of Martin Luther King Jr. and tried to make things better, in a place that needed it most, the world beyond the steps of his own front door. He was by no measure—including his own ambitions—the Martin Luther King *or* the Jackie Robinson of Gulf Coast Alabama. He was a single individual waging a local campaign the best way he could, with the best tools at hand, which included an uncanny instinct, unshakable principles, and a whole lot of love.

Jesse Norwood and Jackie Robinson led parallel, complementary lives. And each suffered a similar premature death. When Jesse Norwood died, much of Mobile's baseball died with him, but just as in the heyday of the Mohawks, who had to move from field to field to field to try to accommodate the throngs of fans who wanted to see them play, there was not a church large enough to accommodate the mourners drawn to his funeral. That, as much as anything else, speaks to the legacy of the man, the impact he had on an entire, beloved community.

Nine

"So now here we are," Councilman Fred Richardson says, back at the Trinity Gardens Recreation Center, a facility built only because of the model of Jesse Norwood and his Mohawk Park, built on the periphery of the remnants of that park. "After all of that, what does it all mean? What do we do now?"

Where do we go from here? King had asked, confronting the seismic shift in his civil rights efforts in the late '60s and facing his own imminent martyrdom wide-eyed and ready. "I don't know if I'll see all of you before April," he told his staff in January of 1968, planning the Poor People's march later in the year, planning a return to Memphis. "I send you forth," he instructed them at the end of their retreat, "as Jesus said to his disciples: Be ye as strong and as tough as a serpent, and tender as a dove."[158]

"Amen," Reverend Willie Lomax says, remembering, perhaps, Mr. Jesse's similarly prophetic words, when he told him he didn't think he had long to live and encouraged Willie to go into coaching.

Jesse Norwood Jr. stands at the front of the room.

There's an old team photo propped up on an easel off to the side. He'd had a difficult time scrounging up photos or other paraphernalia for the occasion, what with the destruction of everything back at the original "homestead," as he calls the house at 1609 Bullshead. There's talk of other photographs out there, even an old uniform, probably a jacket.

"I bet Sleepy's got some of that stuff," Pugh says.

Willie "Sleepy" Burns had all but managed the team in its last year. He'd even tried to put together an older, all-star team of former players in the early '70s. Some say it's the disappointment of not being able to hold the team together that kept him from attending this function.

"Sleepy tried," Lomax says.

The photograph is an informal replica of the classic team pose. A row of six players stands behind another row of six taking a knee. The original was not completely focused, and the enlarged reproduction is extra blurry and grainy. It looks like a hurried, spontaneous effort, allowing for the blurriness, the bad light, the players only agreeing to stop for a moment before they take the field. Their uniforms are clean, and you can make out the anticipation and joy in their faces, even if you can't see the details of their features.

There's a gap in the back row left of center, where a thirteenth player didn't quite settle into place before the others urged the photographer to "Hurry up, shoot, man." They had a game to play.

To the right of center of that same row another player has managed to just step into the arrangement, his shoulders not yet square to the camera. To his left stands "Shoe" Lomax, bearded and smiling. This is a mature picture, judging from Shoe's facial hair, the relative thickness of his waist. He's the only one wearing one of their cherished jackets, which probably means he's slated to pitch that day, and is keeping his arms covered, and warm. He's looking to the side of the lens, either looking beyond baseball, or just beyond this obligatory function, thinking about his pitch sequence.

To Lomax's left is probably Sleepy, though no one can say for sure, the picture is especially fuzzy and dark at the edges. Tall, solid, hands on his hips in the posture of a patient mentor—"That has to be Sleepy," Jack Tillman says, though his insistence may just be the result of the haunting memory of his first encounter with Burns.

They place the year of the photo as no earlier than 1965, because the Candyman is *not* in the picture, not at the center of things.

"I can't make out who that is," May says of the player kneeling in the center front row with a pair of bats crisscrossed before him. His hat is pulled down low on his forehead and the shadow of its bill obscures most of his face. "Jasper?"

Whichever player it is, to his left is Emanuel, so it has to be in the middle of the year, a summer month when he would have been able to get away from school. He is pitched forward in his crouch, ready to spring into action, grinning a Cheshire cat grin. "Yeah, I know what you got" is the message the look transmits. "I know all about you, and I'm ready. Let's go."

On the other side of center kneels Pugh, just as ready, but his posture is typically loose and relaxed. Where Emanuel exudes an attitude of eagerness to get on with it, Pugh's is laid-back, as if murmuring, "Go on. Bring it."

To Pugh's right, Sam Madison genuflects in a cobra coil, his explosive power evident in his thick, bare arms, crossed at the wrists and resting on his raised left knee. A white hand towel is draped over that knee, which he'll use to keep his hands dry so they won't slip when he swings his mighty bat. Sam holds his ball cap off his head, in his left hand. He and Lomax are the only ones bareheaded, but Madison is looking straight into the camera, "Dead red," as Ellis May says.

They are behind the backstop, and you can only make out a corner of foul territory behind home plate, but you can see in the background a stripe of sidewalk and cars already lined up at the curb, the crowd gathering for another Prichard Mohawks baseball game.

"Oh, this is bringing back some good memories," Jimmy Knight says.

He had been reluctant to be interviewed years earlier, reluctant, or just too busy in his work within the school system to find the time to talk about an era as dated and fuzzy as that photograph.

"I probably won't remember much," he'd said when I was finally able to contact him at his office. "I'm sixty years old," he offered, though age had nothing to do with it. His attention had been overwhelmed with the problems of the school system since he first entered it in 1966, the shortages of space and funds, the kids lost to drugs. "I don't know if I'll be able to tell you much of anything."

He gave me ten minutes that afternoon in his office in downtown Mobile's Barton Academy, where the school board is housed. The building, the first academy in the state, dates back to before the Civil War. It was used as a hospital by Union forces after they'd taken Mobile, after Farragut fought his way up Mobile Bay, damning the "torpedos," cannon fire from Forts Morgan and Gaines, which flank the mouth of the bay; after the last battle of the war at Blakeley, which occurred weeks after the official cessation of hostilities at Appomattox. At the end of those ten minutes, beyond the limit, his secretary buzzing in more than once to remind him of his next appointment, it came to him late, like news that the war was over, that the story of the Mohawks ought to be told, the story of baseball at that time ought to be revisited, and we scheduled another interview, over lunch the next week, away from the office. "This is bringing back some *good* memories," he said then, as now.

But where do we go from here?

The first step in an attempt to answer such a question lies in turning from that grainy, dark, and blurry picture to those same faces forty years later. There sits Sam Madison, still poised and content, content that he had at long last discovered himself after falling about as far as you can fall. When he said, "I wouldn't be alive today if it wasn't for Mr. Jesse Norwood," he wasn't talking about the baseball skills he learned from the man, or specific baseball experiences during his time as a Mohawk, I've come to realize. It was Jesse's lesson about being in the right place, delivered all those years ago while on the baseball diamond, that flared through Sam's mind twenty years after the fact, that saved him. He's a coach now, of mighty-mite football in Trinity Gardens, and teaches love.

There sits Reverend Robert Emanuel Jr., still eager to get in on the action, to lead. He has his big, beautiful church down on St. Stephens Road, staying the course in Prichard, Alabama, vocal captain of his congregation, leading them toward a right way of living.

Standing to the side, away from Jesse Norwood Jr. at the lectern, away from the spotlight, is Reverend Willie "Shoe" Lomax, still bearded, the whiskers just another manifestation of his quietness, his words muted somewhat as they pass his covered lips. Unless you were told, you'd never guess he was a Baptist minister. There is nothing about him to indicate the customary fire and brimstone you'd expect from those pulpits. He is a studious man, with a doctorate of men's souls. He grew from a young boy, gangly and ill-fitted, who didn't know the power in his arm, his ability to make a difference, didn't even have his own shoes. He spent years between baseball and the sanctuary walking the streets of Prichard as a meter reader for Alabama Power Company, connecting with people.

And there's Lyonel Pugh. He could do anything on the ball field: defend his position, hit, hit for power, run the bases. Anything. Whatever was needed. He is much the same off the field, moving easily from coaching the Apaches to chauffeuring Mr. Jesse around the region, working in a Brookley warehouse and as an executive for International Paper, from which he retired.

Dead red in the middle of it all sits Ellis "Candyman" May. "I'm still a workaholic," he says, proudly. "I retired once, then got this job. But you know everywhere I've gone, I've been the president," he adds, raising another of those soft rolling chuckles out of Pugh. "It's true," he insists. "Thanks to Mr. Jesse Norwood."

"Whatever you say, Mr. President."

"He taught me *many* things," May says, leaning back in his chair, assuming a posture and delivery more like a preacher than a city foreman. "Taught me to learn many *varied* trades. And I did. And I thank your daddy for that."

Jesse Norwood Jr. grins over at May. He would become mayor of Prichard, of course, but not before college, professional football, not before replicating his father's efforts with the formation of a semipro football team back in his hometown, the Mobile Generals, in the late seventies, where he groomed young men in his preferred sport, some all the way to the professional ranks.

"But I couldn't do it but a few years," he said on another occasion, riding through Prichard, visiting the different Mohawk sites, homes of the players, in his maroon sedan. "That's something else about my father that's important," he said, interrupting the tour at regular intervals, even though at the very beginning of the project he insisted it wasn't a story *about* his father. "He stayed on the front lines a lot longer than most. The lifespan of community service is two, three years. I see that in my work. He was one of those old warhorses, on the battleground fourteen, fifteen years."

Jesse Jr. just fought the battle in different ways. By those years of his tenure with the Generals, Prichard had incorporated itself apart from the city of Mobile but never found its fiscal or municipal footing and soon ranked as one of the poorest communities in the country, despite everyone's effort. Jesse then decided to take the point position of the battle, eventually becoming the city's mayor. It was during his administration that the federal government was convinced to build an interstate spur through the community rather than bypass it, a negotiation that is credited with saving the city. And then he built on that success, securing funding for the establishment of Africatown, an African-American heritage site near the riverfront.

"That's another thing my father taught us: Never forget where you came from."

Jesse has, by this day, grown comfortable with the notion that this story is indeed very much about his father. In response to his initial protests over what I perceived as the focus of the story, I'd told him about my interview with Reverend Emanuel. When asked an introductory question about Jesse Norwood and the Mohawks, Emanuel corrected me by saying, "Jesse Norwood *is* the Mohawks," and then wouldn't say anything else until that distinction was clearly understood.

"That helps," Jesse allowed. "I'm glad Emanuel said that and not me."

"Dead red, Reverend Emanuel, dead red," May says.

But it's a point Jesse had already, if unintentionally, conceded years earlier, during that initial interview, listing off the different men who had come through the Mohawks organization, the positive things they've done with their lives. "I come to realize," he said, "that just about every person who came in contact with my father turned out well, turned out very well. Now that didn't just happen, did it?"

That said, how they got here, where do they go now?

"We're going to start up a foundation, the Mohawk Foundation," Jesse tells them. "And we're taking it back into the community, back to the kids. We're going to build on my father's ideas, his model."

"You talking about putting together another ball club?" Pugh asks, without moving. The question is tinged with weariness, here in his twilight years, as if he's really considering putting on a uniform again, but ready, nonetheless.

Campbell takes a step forward, volunteering for service. He has already said he's game.

"No, no," Jesse tells them, and then hesitates. "Hell, I don't know. Maybe we will."

"Now you're talking," Madison says.

The idea Jesse's talking about, the plan he has in mind, is still in its formative stage. He is talking about centering it around some kind of athletics, maybe baseball, but maybe tennis too; maybe a variety of games. The precise activity isn't as important in his mind yet as the prerequisites that'll go along with the athletics, those of academic achievement and parental involvement, the latter being the most important component of the plan in his eyes. He wants the parents to stake a claim of ownership in the foundation. He talks about it being a foundation "without walls," so that there's never a mistaken notion that what goes on with the foundation is limited to a specific location, pushing instead the idea that those efforts are continuous, lifelong. His father, he says, "knew the separation between substance and ceremony, work and play. But he knew the connection between the two, as well." That's what Jesse is striving to invoke, and inspire, and imitate. That's why this story is so important to him, why he wants to have it told, because he now knows it is so much more than a baseball story.

Conceptually, the roots of his idea go back a lot farther than mid-twentieth-century Alabama. They go all the way back to ancient Greece. Giamatti locates those roots in the Greek word for leisure, *scholē*, the same Greek word that gives us *school*. "What they had in mind as free time survives in what we still appropriately call the liberal arts," he writes, referring "to the classical concept of leisure as being at one with classical and, hence, modern theories of education, not so much in terms of subject matter as in purpose." Giamatti makes the connection between "pure play and schooling that pursues knowledge for its own sake, and leisure or free time."[159]

What connects them all is that they are *autotelic* activities, "that is, their goal is the full exercise of themselves, for their own sake, because in them a condition is achieved that is active, not idle; entertaining, not simply useful; perfecting of our humanity, not merely exploitative of it."[160]

Baseball, simply, inarguably, especially as it was played in the old Negro Leagues, and as it was played by the Prichard Mohawks, is the clearest, most succinct example of the kind of activity Giamatti is essaying. "It was the thing to do," all of those ballplayers say. No one thought of *not* playing baseball, in fact. But why?

I asked Mayor Norwood that question at one of our earliest meetings. We were sitting at a table in the Plateau Elks Lodge, over plates of ribs, discussing this story at a time when neither of us had any idea how much more the story would encompass, though we probably should have. The Plateau Elks Lodge is a converted two-story house, a conversion that didn't make any attempts to disguise the "homestead" it used to be, only expanded its utility, rather, by knocking down some internal walls to provide open space for meetings, dancing, shooting pool, and serving up some of the best barbecued ribs to be found in the city. We should have known, given the symbolic reformation of the dwelling, and its proximity to the I-165 spur, Billy Williams's house, and the Africatown bridge which spans one of Jesse's most cherished achievements from his time as mayor. Africatown is located at a spot on the Mobile River where the *Clothilde*, the last slave ship to dock on American shores in 1859, was subsequently burned and sunk. We should have known.

"What my father saw in the game of baseball was

a love for the game, for playing, in those boys out there in that street, a love for the game, rather than a way out of the ghetto, or a way to make a living. He simply built on what was already there, the love for the game. I think it was only after he had built up the organization that he came to realize that not only was the game fun for them, it taught them discipline they might not have gotten elsewhere, and that would help them improve their lives long after they quit playing. I don't know. We're talking about a man who had no formal education," Jesse said. "I think he was mostly concerned that those kids have a chance to do something they loved, for themselves. He saw a need to facilitate some kind of arena for them when there was so little else, something they could take joy in doing, pride in having done well. If they learned something else from the experience, something about life, that would benefit them later in life, great. But at first, it was all about baseball."

What Jesse's father and the Mohawks achieved on the field anticipated Giamatti's exposition, and even resonated with King's belief that the human soul, all human souls, were divided into sacred and secular realms that flowed in and out of each other, a fundamental duality of life that infused every aspect of being. The precise name for that divide has taken many forms over the centuries, from Cartesian duality, to Hegelian dialectics, and even resides for a time in DuBois's "twoness," the double-consciousness he decries, hoping, pleading for a time when it would become possible to be both Negro and American, without being cursed and spit upon, without having the doors of opportunity slammed in his face.

Thirty-five years after King's assassination, Debra Dickerson writes that it's time to refigure King's and Du Bois's double-consciousness. Being American no longer means absorbing idealized white norms as the unexamined baseline for all behavior. Individual blacks, she says, "need to free their minds, that last plantation, of misleading comparisons and focus instead on self-actualization. For the confused or the cowardly, it's perhaps better to pretend not to be playing the game at all. Best to pretend one is prevented from playing the game, when the reality is that no one can stop the American, black or blind, who is determined to succeed. He can stop, but he cannot *be* stopped. Blacks may not be loved, but they cannot be denied, and it is long past time that black naysayers stopped telling them otherwise."[161]

As for the other, Negro, half, in a book she says is specific to the American experience of slavery and its aftermath, she cites Albert Murray, writing at the time of Jesse Norwood's death: "[S]omeone must at least begin to try to do justice to what U.S. Negroes like about being black and to what they like about being *Americans*. Otherwise justice can hardly be done to the incontestable fact that not only do they choose to live rather than commit suicide, but that, poverty and injustice notwithstanding, far from simply struggling in despair, they live with gusto and a sense of elegance that has always been downright enviable."[162]

It is not an easy agenda, both Murray and Dickerson admit. The notion that the individual who is determined to succeed cannot be stopped is a difficult one to grasp for that individual faced with the discrepancies between starting points on that journey to success. For whatever reason, Kennedy's affirmative action, or Johnson's simple aim to legislate an equitable starting line, has not been accepted as the best method for solving that dilemma. The flaw in that approach manifests itself when you get down to the individual level that Dickerson is addressing, where there will always be a discrepancy. And it is at that individual level, where he imparted that notion that a person determined to succeed cannot be stopped simply by not letting those boys who collected beyond his stoop fail, that Jesse Norwood had his greatest success. The men gathered together in the Trinity Gardens Recreation Center are testimony to that.

"What I'm talking about," Jesse Norwood Jr. says, "with this foundation, is carrying on that legacy, taking the lesson and model of your success out into the street, out to the ballpark, into the classroom," he says, sounding like he's on the stump again, "wherever we need to go to reach today's kids, to show them that it *is* possible to choose not to commit suicide, by killing each other or smoking dope, that they have a choice to live that life of gusto and elegance."

"Step through that door," Campbell says from the back of the room.

"That's right," Jesse tells them. "You remember those lessons," he says, and they all nod, yes. "You got to be prepared, he told me, my brother and sister, just like he told you all, for that door to open. And we've all done that; we've stepped through our doors. But he also said, remember, that we have to hold it open, 'Hold the damn door open,' he'd say to me over and over again, '*Hold* it open!' for others to follow. And the only way to do that is to be confident in who you are, what you are, and never forget where you came from. That's what *I* learned from him, and I think that was the lesson he gave to you as Mohawks."

"And we *thought* we was just playing baseball," Pugh drawls, cackling over the end of his comment, provoking similar responses from some of the others.

Madison says, "Took me *forever* to figure that out," to even more laughter.

Bullshead is paved now. Randolph's store is long gone, as is the mighty oak that once shaded the property. A sedate cedar tree is all that stands on the lot. Melvin Norwood lives alone in 1609. Much has changed, for better and worse. James Harris has recently passed, and though no relation, Bennie

Harris lives a life, because of his heart, on the brink. Jimmy Knight doesn't quite know how to deal with the drug and the dropout problems in today's schools, but agrees that any effort is better than none, and is willing to lend his support to Jesse's Mohawk Foundation, as are all of the former Mohawks, along with the current politicians, Fred Richardson and Sam Jones.

And James "Popcorn" Campbell, who, Jones said, took Jesse Norwood's death hardest of anyone, owns a record store on St. Stephens road, specializing in the blues, promoting local talent. It keeps him busy, he says, but he too stands ready, nonetheless, to pitch in, to play ball. The store, the Music Box, is located no more than three hundred feet, about the distance to the outfield fence of any legitimate ball field, from the back door of 1609 Bullshead, where it all started.

"He was a great, smart man," Ellis May says, solemnly.

"Not bad for only a sixth-grade education, eh?" Jesse asks.

No, not bad at all.

"Here's to you, Mr. Jesse Norwood," Candyman says, raising a glass that is not there, though it is the sentiment, the deserved sentiment, that counts, and the rest of them copy the gesture.

And here's to you, Jackie Robinson, for making it all somehow possible, realizable.

Epilogue

*T*his project began across the desk in the office of the mayor of Prichard, Alabama, across a virtual color line, the Honorable Jesse Norwood Jr., asking a white graduate student if he'd be interested in writing the story. I had written an article for *Mobile Bay Monthly* about the utterly amazing, though seemingly little-known, baseball history of Mobile. Jesse saw the article, tracked me down through the magazine and the university, sat me down in his office, and said, "If you like baseball, *I've* got a baseball story for you."

This was in June of 1993, the same year *Birth of a Fan* was published, a collection of essays by some of America's best writers about baseball, and more: As editor Ron Fimrite writes in his introduction to *Birth*, "It's my guess that the essayists represented here—this one, certainly—were more than a little surprised to find that, in recounting their baseball beginnings, they found much else to ponder. Baseball, it develops, did not merely transform these writers into terminal fans; it also heightened their awareness of a larger world, introduced them to a life beyond childhood" (viii).

In trying to adequately recount the story of Jesse Norwood and his Prichard Mohawks, I found myself tracing threads I never would have expected to be connected to baseball. And yet, if I followed those threads far enough, they always led me back to the game. Like tracking the threads on a baseball itself, there's no beginning, and no end: The stitches both hold it together and keep it in motion, the disparate threads of history and religion, civil rights and parliamentary procedure, always winding back to the game, the object, baseball.

Many of the essays included in *Birth of a Fan*, by male and female contributors, find their way to discussions of fathers or father figures, as agents of the first steps of that introduction to the game of baseball, and by extension to mothers, whose more difficult task it was to let their children—in most cases when they were still just boys in age—loose to follow that path. I wonder if it wasn't easier for those mothers to let go of their grasp on their adolescent children because baseball remains so eternally and obviously a *game* played by men in boy's clothing.

When I started on the actual writing, after many, many delightful hours interviewing these former ballplayers, I set a baseball on my work desk, wherever I happened to be, and convinced myself it was the game ball awarded to my son after one of his more exceptional performances for his Little League team. He played catcher, then—his baseball "career" started

in 1993, too, but by 2000 he'd moved on to swimming, scouts, and the saxophone—and some of my
proudest moments during those years were spent
detailing Joseph's heroics over the telephone for my
father, fourteen hundred miles away in Syracuse, New
York. Dad was a catcher for his college team at Ithaca
(played the sax, too). He introduced me to baseball, in
mostly the usual ways—having a catch on a summer
weekend afternoon, long, hot nights at the Little
League field. But I also remember—a memory as vivid
as any other baseball memory—trips to New York
City, which always included a pilgrimage to the
Bronx, and Yankee Stadium, regardless of the season.
He just wanted to look. "Look," he'd say, every time,
and always with the same reverence, when we'd first
glimpse the stadium, or the green paradise inside.
"Just look."

Earlier in the month that I write this, I had the
opportunity to take someone to her very first major
league baseball game, someone very dear to me and
close to this project, along with two other friends and
writers. It was in Atlanta, Turner Field. As we passed
through the gates and were approaching the concession stand for obligatory hot dogs and beer, Tom
Franklin, a longtime baseball aficionado, stopped us
where we could first see the field, the perfect green
expanse shining under bright lights, and said, "Look,"
an unexpected but perfect example of how this
project came together.

On another occasion Tom wrote to me, after being seized by remembrances of events from our distant past, trying to address—I think—the fleeting yet indelible nature of those remembrances, "It all seems like so much consequence and memory now, when at the time it was so much more; it was possibility." And I think he is correct, though I disagree that it necessarily has to carry that burden of forfeiture, that Proustian, "My God, where did the time go?" as my oldest brother, the namesake of *our* father, has characterized it. (Jim was a pretty fair ballplayer himself, and a lefty, to boot.) Because in baseball, there is no clock, so we are not enslaved to the passage of time, and memories do not have to be wedded to consequence. "Baseball memories are seductive," Roger Angell writes in his contribution to *Birth*, "tempting us always toward sweetness and undercomplexity." And maybe that's what we most love about the game.

In a pivotal soliloquy near the end of Kinsella's novel, *Shoeless Joe*, that undercomplexity is likened to the innocence of the child trapped in all of us, longing for that past. "Baseball," Kinsella's character Jerry says, "is the one constant through all the years." Baseball "continually reminds us of what once was"[163]— what once was good, and could be good again.

"The final irony," Ron Fimrite wrote to me near the completion of this project, is that of the top three major American sports, "baseball today has by far the lowest percentage of African-American participants.

Maybe that's because there are too few teams quite like the Mohawks to keep the playground spirit alive."

I suppose that's the reason I kept that baseball on my desk, as a totem of that spirit. It became emblematic of this project as a whole—the weave, the correspondence—something beyond a display item of a proud father. The irreducible fact is, it probably wasn't *the* ball I wanted to believe it was, though that ceased to make any difference a long time ago. It was the story that mattered, the story bound up in those threads and stitches and that aged, scuffed hide.

— Notes —

1. James M. McPherson, ed., *A Sense of History: The Best Writing from the Pages of American Heritage* (New York City: American Heritage, 1985), 562.

2. Leonard Koppett, *The Thinking Fan's Guide to Baseball, Revised Edition (Hall of Fame Edition No. 3)* (Wilmington: Sport Classic Books, 2004), xi.

3. Ibid., 30.

4. Ibid., 17.

5. Roger Kahn, *The Era: 1947-1957, When the Yankees, the Giants, and the Dodgers Ruled the World* (Boston: Ticknor & Fields, 1993), 117.

6. In fact, Joe Cuhaj and Tamra Carraway-Hinckle document in their book, *Baseball in Mobile*, that Mobile is responsible for introducing the game to Cuba. Nemisio Guillo enrolled in Mobile's Spring Hill College on May 16, 1860, and when he graduated four years later, he brought back to the island nation the first baseball and bat, along with his education, and helped organize the country's first team.

7. Donald Hall, *Fathers Playing Catch with Sons: Essays on Sport (Mostly Baseball)* (New York City:

North Point Press, 1984)

8. Stewart Burns, *To the Mountaintop: Martin Luther King Jr.'s Sacred Mission to Save America, 1955-1968* (New York City: HarperCollins, 2004), x.

9. Any association with gambling was a very sensitive subject for Major League Baseball, of course, the memory of what the "Black Sox" scandal almost did to the game, recent enough to make it an incendiary topic. It remains a sensitive subject to this day, obviously, lest we forget the recent, heated debate concerning Pete Rose.

10. Ron Fimrite, personal correspondence.

11. Kahn, *The Era*, 36.

12. Julie Tygiel, *Baseball's Great Experiment: Jackie Robinson and his Legacy* (New York City: Oxford University Press, 1997), .9.

13. Kahn, *The Era*, 149.

14. Ibid.

15. Ibid, 150.

16. Henry Aaron, "The Trailblazer: Jackie Robinson," *Time Magazine*, October 29, 2003.

17. James Baldwin, *The Fire Next Time* (New York City: Dell, 1963), 19.

18. Ibid., 21.

19. Fimrite, personal correspondence.

20. W. E. B. DuBois, *The Souls of Black Folk* (Chicago: A.C. McClurg & Co., 1903)

21. David Falkner, *Great Time Coming: The Life of Jackie Robinson from Baseball to Birmingham* (New

York City; Simon and Schuster, 1995), 257.

22. Roger Kahn, *The Boys of Summer* (New York City: HarperCollins, 1998), xii.

23. There has only been one significant change to the game itself since: the American League's designated-hitter rule, a rule specifically designed to shift the weight of percentages in favor of the offense, which was not uniformly accepted and is still hotly debated thirty years after its inception. Vigorously opposed by the National League, which each year brings new cries for its repeal, the rule is such a trigger point that there has even been a call for a constitutional amendment banning it.

24. Kahn, *The Era*, 275.

25. Ibid.

26. Leonard Koppett, *The Man in the Dugout* (New York City: Crown, 1993), vii.

27. Kahn, *The Era*, 279.

28. Ibid., 276.

29. Ibid., 280.

30. Ibid.

31. Ibid., 269.

32. Ibid., 278.

33. Koppett, *The Man in the Dugout*, 57.

34. Kahn, *The Era*, 46.

35. Michael Eric Dyson, *I May Not Get There With You: The True Martin Luther King Jr.* (New York City: Touchstone, 2000), 326.

36. Ibid., 63.

37. Kahn, *The Era*, 48.

38. Ibid.

39. Ibid., 52.

40. Ibid., 50.

41. Ibid., 59.

42. Falkner, *Great Time Coming*, 162.

43. Ibid., 14.

44. Tommy Hicks, "Scott Had Eye for Talent," *Mobile Register*, July 25, 2004, 4C.

45. Joe Cuhai and Tamra Carraway-Hinckle, *Baseball in Mobile* (Charleston: Arcadia Publishing, 2003) 77.

46. Baldwin, *The Fire Next Time*, 41.

47. Hicks, "Scott Had Eye for Talent," 4C.

48. Ibid.

49. Kahn, *The Era*, 330.

50. Excerpt *Brown v. Board of Education*.

51. Falkner, *Great Time Coming*, 14.

52. Ibid., 9.

53. Ibid., 10.

54. Ibid., 219

55. Ibid.

56. Ibid., 233.

57. Ibid., 28.

59. A. Bartlett Giamatti, *Take Time for Paradise: Americans and Their Games* (Quezon City: Summit, 1989)

58. Henry M. Robert, *Robert's Rules of Order Revised* (New York City: Morrow, 1979.)

60. Koppett, *Man in the Dugout*, viii.

61. Ibid., 98.

62. Roger Kahn, *Games We Used to Play* (New York City: Ticknor and Fields, 1992), 32.

63. W. P. Kinsella, *Shoeless Joe* (Boston: Mariner, 1999), 149.

64. Bruce Adelson, *Brushing Back Jim Crow: The Integration of Minor-League Baseball in the American South* (Charlottesville: University of Virginia Press, 1999), 15.

65. Robert Peterson, *Only the Ball Was White* (New York City: Oxford Press, 1992), 16.

66. Michael E. Lomax, *Black Baseball Entrepreneurs* (Syracuse: Syracuse University Press, 2003), 14

67. Peterson, *Only the Ball was White*, 17.

68. Ibid.

69. Lomax, *Black Baseball Entrepreneurs*, 21.

70. Peterson, *Only the Ball Was White*, 17.

71. George Will, *Men At Work* (New York City: Harper Perennial, 1991), 2.

72. Nicholas Dawson, ed., *Baseball: A Literary Anthology* (New York City: The Library of America, 2002), 52.

73. Ibid., 6.

74. Ibid., 5.

75. Ibid.

76. Ibid., 7.

77. Peterson, *Only the Ball Was White*, 46.

78. Ibid.

79. Ibid., 25.

80. Ibid., 43.

81. Ibid., 26.

82. Ibid., 27.

83. Ibid.

84. Ibid., 28.

85. Ibid.

86. Ibid., 39.

87. Ibid., 31.

88. DuBois, *The Souls of Black Folk*, 141.

89. Peterson, *Only the Ball Was White*, 53.

90. Taylor Branch, *Parting the Waters: America in the King years, 1954-1963* (New York City: Simon and Schuster, 1988), 3.

91. Giamatti, *Take Time for Paradise*, 42.

92. Ibid., 33.

93. Ibid.

94. Ibid., 34.

95. Ibid., 35

96. Ibid., 83.

97. Ibid., 63.

98. Burns, *To the Mountaintop*, 111.

99. Ibid., 110.

100. Falkner, *Great Time Coming*, 235.

101. Burns, *To the Mountaintop*, 15.

102. Giamatti, *Take Time for Paradise*, 40.

103. Burns, *To the Mountaintop*, 163.

104. Ibid., 164.

105. Ibid.

106. Falkner, *Great Time Coming*, 79.

107. Ibid., 78.

108. Ibid., 71.

109. Ibid., 72.

110. Ibid.

111. Ibid., 75.

112. Ibid., 132

113. Ibid.

114. Jackie Robinson and Alfred Duckett, *I Never Had It Made: The Autobiography of Jackie Robinson* (New York City: HarperCollins, 1995), 95.

115. Falkner, *Great Time Coming*, 241.

116. Robinson, *I Never Had It Made*, 122.

117. Burns, *To the Mountaintop*, 143.

118. Falkner, *Great Time Coming*, 259.

119. Ibid., 253.

120. Burns, *To the Mountaintop*, 12

121. Ibid, 385.

122. Falkner, *Great Time Coming*, 264.

123. Robinson, *I Never Had It Made*, 7.

124. Ibid., 8.

125. Burns, *To the Mountaintop*, 182.

126. Baldwin, *The Fire Next Time*, 141.

127. Steven Kasher, *The Civil Rights Movement: A Photographic History 1954-1968* (New York City: Abbeville Press, 1996), 6.

128. Falkner, *Great Time Coming*, 302.

129. Burns, *To the Mountaintop*, 390.

130. Ibid.

131. Ibid.

132. Stephen B. Oates, *Let the Trumpet Sound* (New York City: Harper & Row, 1982.)

133. Falkner, *Great Time Coming*, 10.

134. Ibid.

135. Jackie Robinson, *Baseball Has Done It* (Philadelphia: Lippincott, 1964), 11.

136. Tygiel, *Baseball's Great Experiment*, 302.

137. Ibid.

138. Falkner, *Great Time Coming*, 268.

139. Ibid., 315.

140. Burns, *To the Mountaintop*, 128.

141. Ibid., 127.

142. Ibid., 457.

143. Ibid.

144. Dyson, *I May Not Get There with You*, xv.

145. Burns, *To the Mountaintop*, 322.

146. Ibid.

147. Ibid., 349.

148. Ibid., 344.

149. Ibid., 354.

150. Dyson, *I May Not Get There with You*, 12.

151. Falkner, *Great Time Coming*, 330.

152. Ibid., 326.

153. Robinson, *I Never Had It Made*, 226.

154. Ibid., 253.

155. Falkner, *Great Time Coming*, 337.

156. Ibid., 344.

157. Ibid., 341.

158. Burns, *To the Mountaintop*, 385.

159. Giamatti, *Take Time for Paradise*, 27.

160. Ibid., 28.

161. Debra Dickerson, *The End of Blackness* (New York City: Pantheon Books, 2004), 9.

162. Ibid., 6.

163. Kinsella, *Shoeless Joe*, 253.

Acknowledgments

Opportunity, in Eastern thought, is a collective endeavor. It's pulling someone else along with you as you're being led toward possibility, *given* a chance. This book, these few hundred pages, didn't happen without a lot of pulling and pushing. I could easily field a baseball team from those directly responsible. Jesse Norwood Jr., custodian, holder of the story, has to be the first person acknowledged, for without his confidence, his faith, his *belief*, not to mention his tireless effort, this book wouldn't have happened at all. Thank you, Jesse. I would put David Poindexter in the general manager's slot, whose love of baseball and of books made this one possible, in an absolute way, from the title, to your hands. Sonny Brewer, a man of many utilities, resurrected both this writer and this story. Coach Ron Fimrite graciously guided the story along with his knowledge, insight, wisdom and patience. There is no story to write, of course, without the Mohawk players and acquaintances, Emanuel, Lomax, Campbell, Madison, Pugh, Maye, Harris, Jasper, Sellers, Dillard, Freddie Sigler, Selmna Miles, Robert

Rembert, Jimmy Knight, Sam Jones, Jack Tillman, Hattie and Melvin Norwood, and on and on. I owe them more than gratitude. I owe them admiration and respect, just because of who they are and what they did. I can only hope that comes out in these pages. And there was a whole substitute squad ready to pitch in comments and encouragement, willing to sacrifice their time to listen or read: Jim Gilbert-Jim Gilbert (double mention because he was also the procurer of much resource material), Tommy Franklin, John T. Edge, Bev & Butch Marshall, David Wright, Jay Sharpe, Phil Cusa, Pat Murphy, Dave Carner: Thank you, all. As always, thanks to all the great folks at MacAdam/Cage, Scott, Pat, J.P., Dorothy, Melanie, Tasha, Julie, Jason, *et al*— ever-patient professionals, every one of you. Two people deserve special mention, both for their contributions and in lieu of an apology: Through her involvement with this book, Suzanne Hudson is not quite as quick to profess disinclination toward baseball. I'm not sorry for that. And Martin Lanaux, like the best of clubhouse managers, was forever scrounging up old books and magazine articles for the research. Thanks, Mar-ten, even if you do hold me responsible for squandering so much money on your baseball card collection. Thank you, again, Cecelia, Joseph and Sam.